URBAN DWELLING ENVIRONMENTS

an elementary survey of settlements for the study of design determinants

URBAN DWELLING ENVIRONMENTS,

an elementary survey of settlements for the study of design determinants

HORACIO CAMINOS   JOHN F. C. TURNER   JOHN A. STEFFIAN

M.I.T. REPORT NO. 16

THE M.I.T. PRESS

Massachusetts Institute of Technology
Cambridge, Massachusetts, and London, England

ACKNOWLEDGMENTS

This work is part of an education-research program on "Urban Settlements in Developing Countries," carried out at the Massachusetts Institute of Technology in the School of Architecture and Planning.

The program is fully supported by a Ford Foundation International Affairs Grant.

Participants in this program are graduate students in the Department of Architecture who are working in the following combined subjects: Architectural Design, Section C (Caminos, Steffian), Urban Settlements, Squatters and Social Change (Turner).

The material for this work has been gathered during the following periods: Boston, 1966–1968 (Steffian); Lima, Arequipa, 1957–1964 (Turner); Ciudad Guayana, 1965 (Caminos), 1967 (Turner); Medellín, 1966–1968 (Caminos). Preliminary studies were started in the fall of 1966. During the summer of 1967, several Boston cases were tentatively analyzed. In the fall of 1967, surveys and drawings of the sixteen cases shown in this collection were partially developed by the following members of the 1968 graduate class as part of their course work: Christopher Benninger, Daniel Brown, Brooks Cavin, Bruce Creager, Guy Dorian Cristol, Gray Henry, Fernando Ruiz, and Benjamin Smith. The final work was completed in the fall of 1968. All models of the Locality Segments were built by Ignacio Garabieta (M.I.T. Research Associate).

Sources of information are indicated with the plans, diagrams, and charts. In addition, other reference material has come from the following sources: U.S.A.: Boston Redevelopment Authority; Cambridge Corporation and Cambridge Planning Board; Lincoln Planning Board; Anderson, Beckwith and Haible, architects. Peru: Joint Center for Urban Studies of Harvard and M.I.T.; Olivetti Foundation Grant; Junta Nacional de la Vivienda; Oficina del Plano Metropolitano de Lima, Centro de estudios y promoción. Venezuela: Corporación Venezolana de Guayana. Colombia: Municipio de Medellín, Departamento Administrativo de Planeación, Fundación Casitas de la Providencia.

Photographs reproduced in this study are from the following sources. Boston Urban Area: Boston Redevelopment Authority; M.I.T. Department of Architecture, Visual Art Section under a Rockefeller Grant, Nishan Bichajian and students; Cambridge Historical Commission, B. Orr, photography; Aerial photos of New England; Massachusetts Port Authority, Fay Foto Service Inc.; Gray Henry; Bruce Creager; Brooks Cavin; Miguel Caminos. Lima, Arequipa Urban Areas: Servicio Aerofotográfico Nacional of Peru; John F. C. Turner; Foto Art, Eva Lewitus. Ciudad Guayana: John F. C. Turner. Medellín: Rodrigo Arboleda Halaby. Photograph of the Locality Segment models, topography only: Miguel Caminos; with buildings: Robert J. Slattery.

We are indebted to Joan M. Wollner, Mary Jervey, Susan Myers, Christine Cosmopoulos, and Mrs. Marilyn Pierce for the preparation of the manuscript.

We are grateful for personal assistance and advice from the following people: Boston: Don R. Brown; Lima: Diego Robles, Hans Harms, Hélan Jaworski; Ciudad Guayana: Julio A. Silva, Matilde Marquez; Medellín: Rodrigo Arboleda Halaby, Hector Posada.

The authors are deeply grateful to the people and institutions mentioned here as well as to many others who have contributed to this work.

H.C.
J.F.C.T.
J.A.S.

SUMMARY

CONTENT: Comparable sketches of sixteen urban dwelling environments (localities), eight in Boston and eight in four Latin American cities.

Urban Area	Locality
BOSTON, Massachusetts, U.S.A.	EAST BOSTON
	CHARLESTOWN
	NORTH END
	SOUTH END
	WASHINGTON PARK
	COLUMBIA POINT
	CAMBRIDGEPORT, Cambridge, Massachusetts
	LINCOLN, Massachusetts
LIMA, Peru	CUEVAS
	EL ERMITAÑO
	EL AGUSTINO (Hill)
	EL AGUSTINO (Flat)
	MENDOCITA
AREQUIPA, Peru	MARIANO MELGAR
CIUDAD GUAYANA, Venezuela	EL GALLO
MEDELLIN, Colombia	VILLA SOCORRO

Each of the five different urban areas or contexts is summarily outlined in terms of topography, climate, land use, ecology of the income groups, with notes on the economy and demography of the areas.

Each of the sixteen localities or dwelling environments is described in similar terms at four scales: the locality itself, a segment of the locality, a dwelling group, and a typical dwelling unit.

AIMS: (1) To dramatize the correlation between settlements and the geographic and cultural context in the rapidly urbanizing world of today; (2) to illustrate various levels and aspects of the physical environment; (3) to compare and contrast different "products" and their relationship to effective demands; (4) to find a framework for a more comprehensive approach to settlement development and design.

APPLICATION: A rough tool for reference and information for those concerned with the development of urban areas in transitional contexts.

This publication is available in both bound and unbound copies. The unbound version has been prepared so that the drawings or photographs may be displayed and the different environments can be easily compared.

The drawings can be displayed in such a way that vertically, the complete sequence of a case will be seen at every level of study—the Urban Area, Locality, Locality Segment, Dwelling Group, and Dwelling. Horizontally, all the cases can be compared at the same level of study, from the urban areas to the dwellings.

No one really has an honest answer or a consequent action that implies any real hope for the 300 million people of Latin America, whose number will reach 600 million within 25 years and who, although desolately poor in the overwhelming majority, have the right to a material life, to culture, and to civilization.

INTRODUCTION

This collection of surveys is intended as a contribution toward a better understanding of the relationship between people and their dwelling places in the context of rapid social change. The common denominators of the environmental condition and prospect in all regions of the world today are newness, urbanization, increasing control of land use, urban services, building and plant design by government agencies, and implementation of urban development by large-scale organization. Cities are rapidly expanding in size and population, along with the social, political, and economic institutions that produce and maintain them; the area for personal and local control is shrinking; the conflict between environment and human need is growing. Without adequate knowledge of the determining factors, planning of the environment is becoming increasingly superficial, irrelevant, and, in short, impotent to deal with the environmental problems of poverty and of wealth.

Complete change of the man-made environment is in the making, marked by a colossal and ever-increasing demand for shelter. In thirty years the present population will double from 3.4 billion to 6.4 billion, and by that time 80 to 90 per cent of the world population will be urbanized. In Africa, Asia, and South America, as well as in the largely industrialized regions of Europe and North America, the great majority of sons and grandsons of the previous and present generation of peasants will live in environments that bear little resemblance to the traditional village. Radically new forms for cities are being proposed within economies that, in theory at least, could afford to build them. If significant investment priorities change in the coming years, or if modes of communication continue to change as rapidly as they have in the past, the form of future dwelling environments may be as different for the wealthy as for the poor.

Sixteen localities are analyzed in this preliminary survey, along with basic data on population characteristics corresponding to the physical forms described at the times of the surveys. These analyses are no more than catalysts for leading questions about the relationships between socioeconomic contexts, housing demands, and environmental products and no more than raw material for the formulation of hypotheses. The selection was determined from first-hand knowledge and personal experience as well as the availability of data. The variety is sufficiently wide, and the surveys sufficiently detailed, to provoke many questions, to suggest many correlations, to indicate areas for further studies, and to aid those concerned with practical problems in the development of environments.

These studies are based on the premise that the values of things designed and built lie in their relationships to the users and makers and not in any quantifiable characteristics of the isolated object. These studies are, therefore, of surroundings that cannot be identified or evaluated without knowledge of that which is surrounded; studies of habitats or of inhabitants are necessarily studies of areas of relationship between them. As these relationships are functions of different and changing social, economic, and physical circumstances, environmental design for a heterogeneous population is certainly one of the most complex and challenging tasks in the world today.

The life histories of two families, one in Boston and one in Lima, are briefly sketched here to illustrate the differences and correspondences of two contrasting environments. The use of two contrasting contexts makes it easier to focus on a relatively unknown area—that of the relationship between the physical and social systems. The comparison illustrates this area clearly because of the obvious differences between the contexts of a slow-growing industrial city in an economy of abundance and a fast-growing, transitional city in an economy of scarcity.

A third generation of a European immigrant family, born of parents from the "upper-lower" or "skilled, blue-collar" class, is taken as representative of social change in contemporary Boston; a first-generation, rural immigrant family is taken to represent social change in contemporary Lima, the capital of a rapidly urbanizing country, typical of many transitional economies. Mid-twentieth-century Boston is growing relatively slowly and mainly through local population increase; by world standards, regional and metropolitan as well as personal incomes are very high and are rising rapidly. The level of social insurance and services is also high. Contemporary Lima, on the other hand, is growing extremely fast because of high rates of rural-urban immigration and natural increase. The national per capita income is very low, and, though much higher in the metropolitan area of Lima, both city and per capita incomes are still very low by world standards. Consequently the levels of welfare insurance and social service are also very low, especially for the bulk of the wage-earning population. The latter receive little or no sickness or unemployment pay and work under highly competitive labor-market conditions.

There are, however, some important similarities and parallels in the experience of the two families: both undergo a considerable change of social status and geographic location—both exchange central urban for suburban dwelling environments. The important and striking differences in their environments, the sequence of family location changes, and the trajectories of development of these environments correlate with the differences of social characteristics and situations. The families are of significantly different size and structure: the Boston family, though part of a local kinship network in the North End home, is much smaller than the Lima counterpart. The second-generation, nuclear family, is smaller than the previous in both cases but in the Boston case the second-generation family is much less likely to establish or re-establish the extended family structure, even when they become owners of a large and very spacious dwelling. The Lima family builds its house, starting at a much earlier stage in its socioeconomic trajectory, with the intention of providing for future as well as present generations. The Boston family, on the other hand, uses its property investments as equity and maintains a high degree of geographic as well as social mobility. If the Lima family realizes its plan of establishing itself permanently in their (initially squatter) location, this will reflect their ac-

ceptance of a ceiling to their upward mobility. If the later generations wish to establish themselves in the middle class, they would have to move away from the area which is unlikely to improve beyond the upper-lower or lower-middle-class status. In any case, the chances of the second- or even third-generation Lima family moving up into the middle class are relatively remote; because while there is a great deal of upward mobility from the lowest to the upper-lower occupational and income classes, there is less mobility between the lower blue- and white-collar and the upper white-collar classes.

The differences between the qualities of the two families' dwelling environments and the correlation of these contrasts with the differences of personal incomes is obvious. The income difference and effective purchasing power of the Boston family is about ten times greater than the Lima family. The well-established working class family in Lima, with a relatively good income by local standards, is still far below the officially defined poverty line of the United States in terms of consumption levels and living standards.

Comparative judgments on the material merits of the dwellings are bound to the relative differences of incomes and living standards. Over time, each family achieves a considerable improvement of housing conditions within the standards of its own context.

Even the few basic contextual variables described are enough to indicate very different and changing responses each family demands from its dwelling environment. Priorities are easily understood if demands are defined in terms of location, amenity, and tenure and if these demands in turn are interpreted in terms of physical proximity to the sources of socioeconomic livelihood and security, modernity of the dwelling, and permanence of residence. The generally low priorities for location near central urban areas and the high priorities for modern amenities in the Boston case contrast strongly with the Lima counterpart. In a transitional industrially and institutionally under-developed economy, proximity to central areas is essential for those with the lowest incomes and

the least secure employments. Those who have little or no savings margin over and above the minimum expenditure necessary to keep alive, must live in or adjacent to the areas of maximum intensity and diversity of low-income employment and in areas of high population density. Without proximity to central or "inner ring" areas, the poorest and least secure, who can not afford time or cash for commuting, can not achieve their principal objective; that is, to become less poor and more secure. Those who get more skilled, better paid, and more secure work, but who may still slide back into extreme poverty as they are uninsured against illness and unemployment, are less dependent on geographic proximity but far more dependent on the permanent possession of their homes. This is a partial substitute, at least, for the loss of the traditional security of the local kinship network (which is lost when the immigrant leaves his home and which takes several generations to re-establish in the urban context) and the inaccessibility of institutionalized insurance, enjoyed only by the relatively wealthy. The possessor of an urban homestead, even if it is no more than a shack on a plot of unserviced land, can rent a part or can use it as a shop or workshop. Not only can he reduce his expenditure by the 20 per cent or more demanded by minimum rents for an urban tenement slum, and so avoid the constant threat of eviction, but the home-site-owning family can increase its savings or its income in time of need by renting part or by using part as a shop or workshop. The savings will, in general, be invested in the construction by stages of a permanent dwelling with modern standards, without undermining security of tenure with a mortgage. After the ten or fifteen years necessary for the completion of the first unit of their dwelling have elapsed, the average family has a higher priority for modern amenities and a lower priority for permanent tenure. This is likely to happen when the income of the household is higher and securer because the principal earner will have reached the peak of his skill, and the older children, or the less burdened mother, may also be working. More important at this later stage will be the social status given by the quality of the dwelling environment and the social security given by its equity value rather than by the inalienability of its tenure.

With the very great differences of income level and social and economic security provided by a wealthy and expanding economy, the priorities of the Boston family are clearly different. Only the older generation, firmly established in a relatively stable, local community and with many relatives in the immediate neighborhood, is likely to give a higher priority to location and permanent tenure than to modern amenities. With a steadily shrinking supply of apartments for reasonable rents in an area such as the North End of Boston, young newlyweds are more likely to look for homes of their own in other parts of the city. The higher the aspirations of the younger generation in relation to the status of their parents, the less tolerant will they be of traditional extended family ties and the relatively static social environment of the stable community. The high-school and university-educated children of blue-collar-class parents will demand more personal independence and more space than they are likely to find in or near the family home. As aspirants to what they and their society regard as higher social levels, the young generation will feel somewhat insecure, culturally or psychologically speaking, and will therefore be particularly anxious to exhibit the newly acquired styles of the groups with whom they identify. With a greatly reduced economic and social dependence on the local kinship group and with relatively high and assured incomes at all stages of life, the typical nuclear family in modern society chooses its dwelling environment in accordance with the closely interrelated demands of physical comfort and social status. These are much more likely to determine location and tenure than to determine the levels of amenity.

These cases suggest a hypothesis to explain the difference between the social ecology of U.S. cities and the Latin American ones. The lowest income sectors in Boston are concentrated in central areas, while in the latter cases they are to be found on the periphery also. In the case of the larger Latin American cities this would be due to "suburbanization" at a rela-

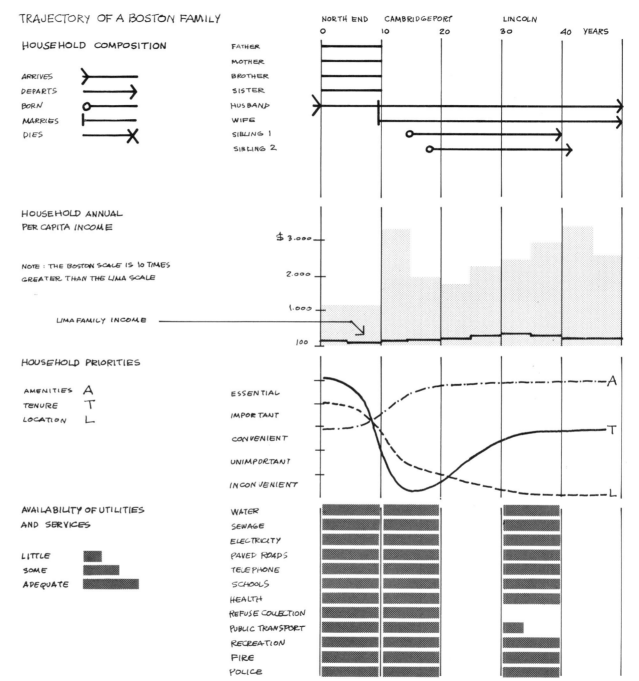

TRAJECTORY OF A LIMA FAMILY

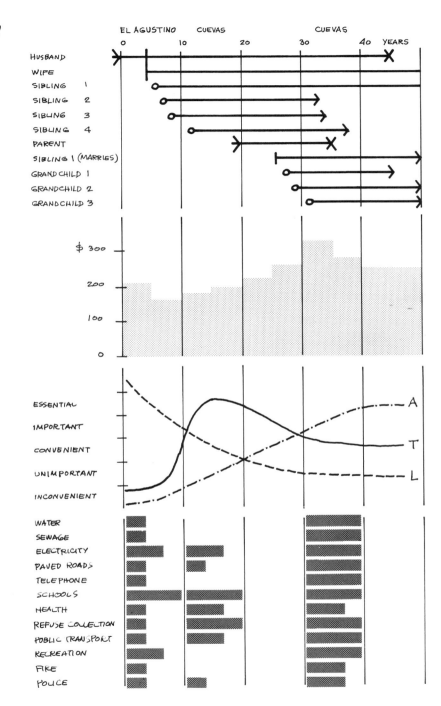

HOUSEHOLD COMPOSITION

ARRIVES
DEPARTS
BORN
MARRIES
DIES

HOUSEHOLD ANNUAL
PER CAPITA INCOME

NOTE: THE BOSTON SCALE IS 10 TIMES
GREATER THAN THE LIMA SCALE

HOUSEHOLD PRIORITIES

AMENITIES   A
TENURE   T
LOCATION   L

AVAILABILITY OF UTILITIES
AND SERVICES

LITTLE
SOME
ADEQUATE

tively earlier stage of socioeconomic change, that is, if the above case is really representative. The search for permanent tenure on the part of the Lima family at an early stage of its trajectory points to another and complementary contrast: families in modern industrial and post-industrial society are increasingly mobile and generally change their urban geographic locations with every major change of occupation and social location or status. Unlike the Boston family, the Lima counterpart achieves or maintains upward social mobility by virtue of its geographic stability. The family achieves an environment of a higher status by improving its property, without necessarily changing location. It is only at the successful conclusion of the latter's trajectory that the two sets of priorities and consequently the forms of their environments begin to coincide.

The accompanying sets of charts illustrate the life trajectories of the two families in Boston and in Lima. The charts show, comparatively, how different factors change in time: household composition, income, priorities, availability of utilities and services. The Boston family moves through different localities represented by the North End, Cambridgeport, Lincoln. The Lima family moves through different localities represented by El Agustino, Cuevas. The families are not actual case studies but rather representative of characteristic patterns of life in Boston and Lima.

Horacio Caminos
John F. C. Turner
John A. Steffian
November 1968
Cambridge, Massachusetts

EXPLANATORY NOTES

Locality: A locality is defined as a relatively self-contained residential area within an urban context. In general, it is contained within physical boundaries that are of two types: barriers and meshing boundaries. Mountains, water, limited-access highways and sharp changes in land use are considered barriers. Main streets and political, or municipal, divisions are considered meshing boundaries.

Locality segment: All the localities differ, especially in size and shape. A segment of the same dimension has been taken from each locality for purposes of comparison. The size of the segment is 400 meters by 400 meters (approximately 1/4 mile by 1/4 mile) or a six-minute walk.

Block: Within each locality segment a primarily residential block has been selected to allow comparison of areas and densities that are homogeneous. The block is bounded on all sides by circulation so that the ratio of circulation (or service) to area served can be compared.

Dwelling group: The dwelling group serves to establish the context for the dwelling in its immediate environment.

Dwelling: The dwelling is a self-contained unit that can be an apartment, row house, or detached house for one or more families.

Progressive Development: The construction of the dwelling and the development of local infrastructure to modern standards by stages, often starting with provisional structures and underdeveloped land. This essentially traditional procedure is generally practiced by squatters who have de facto security of tenure and adequate building sites.

Instant Development: The modern procedure in which all structures and services are completed before occupation.

The information given in drawings, charts and descriptions has been qualified in the following manner:

Tentative: When based upon rough estimation of limited sources

Approximate: When deducted from different sources

Accurate: When taken from reliable sources

Symbols and Labels on Circulation Plans

Vehicular: Solid lines of different thicknesses represent vehicular circulation at different levels of intensity (number of vehicles over time): *light, medium, heavy.*

Pedestrian: Dots differently spaced represent pedestrian circulation at different levels of intensity (number of people over time): *few, some, many.*

Local: Street or avenue used mainly by locality traffic.

Vicinal: Street or avenue used mainly by traffic to and from areas adjacent to the locality.

Through: Avenue or limited-access highway used mainly by outside traffic.

Rapid Transit Lines or MBTA (Massachusetts Bay Transportation Authority): A mass transportation service (street cars and/or subways and/or elevated lines) provided by the MBTA.

Construction Types Charts

The main dwelling construction types were grouped as follows:

Shack

  Roof Mats, tin, cardboard, wood crating, etc.
  Walls Mats, tin, cardboard, wood crating, etc.
  Floor Earth

Adobe

  Roof Wood frame with mud or asbestos or terracotta tiles
  Walls Adobe
  Floor Earth or slab-on-grade

Wood

  Roof Wood joists with shingles or tar and gravel
  Walls Wood frame
  Floor Wood joists with wood subfloor

Wood and Masonry

  Roof Wood joists with shingles or tar and gravel
  Walls Brick, block, or tile masonry without columns
  Floor Wood joists with wood subfloor

Masonry and Concrete

  Roof Poured or precast concrete with tar and gravel
  Walls Brick, block, or tile masonry without columns
  Floor Poured, precast or slab-on-grade concrete

Concrete

  Roof Poured or precast concrete with tar and gravel
  Walls Masonry with columns or reinforced concrete
  Floor Poured and/or precast concrete

Metric System Equivalents

Linear Measures

1 centimeter		= 0.3937 inches
1 meter	= 100 centimeters	= 39.37 inches or 3.28 feet
1 kilometer	= 1,000 meters	= 3,280.83 feet or 0.62137 miles
1 inch		= 2.54 centimeters
1 foot		= 0.3048 meters
1 mile		= 1.60935 kilometers

Square measures

1 square meter		= 1,550 square inches or 10,7639 square feet
1 hectare	= 10,000 square meters	= 2.4711 acres
1 square foot		= 0.0929 square meters
1 acre		= 0.4087 hectare

Dollar Equivalents

All income data have been expressed in terms of the U.S. equivalent; the exchange rates at the periods referred to were as follows per one U.S. dollar:

26.80 Peruvian Soles
 4.50 Venezuelan Bolivares
15.00 Colombian Pesos

PRINCIPAL SOURCES AND ABBREVIATIONS

BOSTON, Massachusetts, U.S.A.

B.R.A. Boston Redevelopment Authority, Boston, Massachusetts.

B.H.A. Boston Housing Authority, Boston, Massachusetts.

Hipshman, May B. *Public Housing at the Crossroads: The Boston Housing Authority.* Advisory Committee, Boston Housing Authority, Citizens Housing and Planning Association, Boston, 1967.

J.C.U.S. Joint Center for Urban Studies of M.I.T. and Harvard University. *Planning Metropolitan Boston.* Metropolitan Area Planning Council and J.C.U.S., 1967.

Rodwin, Lloyd. *Housing and Economic Progress:* a study of the housing experiences of Boston's middle-income families. The M.I.T. Press, Cambridge, 1961.

Warner, Sam B. *Streetcar Suburbs:* the process of growth in Boston 1870–1900. The M.I.T. Press, Cambridge, 1962.

Whitehill, Walter Muir. BOSTON: *A Topographical History.* Harvard University Press, Cambridge, 1968.

LIMA, AREQUIPA, Peru

Caravedo, B., Rotondo, H., and Mariategui, J. *Estudios de Psiquiatria Social en el Peru.* Ediciones del Sol, Lima, 1963.

Koth de Paredes, Marcia, and Turner, John F. C. Field studies carried out under the auspices of the J.C.U.S. and the Olivetti Foundation. Lima, 1965.

J.N.V. Junta Nacional de la Vivienda, Lima, Peru.

O.A.T.A. Oficina de Asistencia Técnica de Arequipa, Ministerio de Obras Públicas, Lima.

Pattison, W. H. Ralph. *Urbanización Popular; Lima 1965.* Unpublished dissertation, Faculty of Architecture, University of Newcastle upon Tyne, 1967.

S.A.N. Servicio Aereofotográfico Nacional del Peru, Lima, Peru.

U.N.S.M. Universidad Nacional de San Marcos, Lima, Peru. *Investigacion de la Barriada el Ermitaño.* 1965.

D.E.S.C.O. Centro de Estudios y Promoción del Desarrollo, Lima, Peru.

CIUDAD GUAYANA, Venezuela

C.S.E.D. Center for Studies of Education and Development, Harvard University.

C.V.G. Corporacion Venezolana de Guayana. *The Guayana Economic Program Key to the Development of Venezuela.* Cambridge, J.C.U.S., 1967.

Silva, Julio A. *Programa de Mejoramiento Urbano Progresivo para Areas de Recepcion en Ciudad Guayana.* Ciudad Guayana, Fundación de la Vivienda del Caroní, 1967.

MEDELLIN, Colombia

Departamento Administrativo de Planeación Municipal, Medellín.

Fundación Casitas de la Providencia, Medellín.

Instituto de Crédito Territorial, Bogotá, 1964.

CONTENTS

1. URBAN AREAS

BOSTON, Massachusetts, U.S.A.

1. The city is located at the head of the Massachusetts Bay, latitude 42° North, longitude 71° West. Summer and winter temperatures range between the extremes of —18° C. and 38° C.; there is precipitation all year around with monthly averages ranging between 10 and 40 centimeters, often accompanied by high winds. Boston is the only one of the urban areas with below-zero temperatures and snow.

2. The Shawmut peninsula, now mainly occupied by the central business district, was originally settled by the Massachusetts Bay Company in 1630, then "a necke and bare of wood (and free from) the three great annoyances of Woolves, Rattlesnakes and Musketoes." By the 1660's, almost all importations from England were handled by Boston Merchants, and the town was the principal center of the Colonies until the 1740's. Exceptionally prosperous until the mid-nineteenth century, Boston's economy was supported by shipbuilding, textiles, and manufacturing. From the start Boston has been a center of intellectual life: Harvard University was founded in 1636, and the first American newspaper in 1704.

3. Boston is a major financial center; principal industries include publishing, food-processing, shoe and textile production, machinery, and, most recently and most importantly, electronics. Over-all employment has grown substantially less, but productivity increased substantially more than the national average. The gross per capita income for Boston in 1963 was U.S. $2,800 annually, against the GNP of U.S.$3,000.

4. The Boston Standard Metropolitan Area is composed of 65 small, independent but adjacent towns and cities. The city government of Boston exercises its authority over 25 per cent of the metropolitan population. Authorities with metropolitan spheres of action include the Police Department, the Massachusetts Department of Public Works, and the Massachusetts Bay Transportation Authority. All local building controls and codes are exercised by local governments.

5. The politically defined city of Boston reached its peak population in 1950; by that year it was only the central part of the metropolitan area and represented 36 per cent of the total. By 1963, the city population had decreased by approximately one sixth, leaving the city with only one quarter of the metropolitan population—and a very high proportion of the lowest income and ethnic minority groups. The national population growth rate, in 1963, was 1.69 per cent, and that of the Boston metropolitan area approximately 2 per cent. Boston, therefore, is a relatively slow growing urban area in the context of the U.S.A. and very slow by comparison with most countries in Latin America. Thirty-five per cent of the 1960 population was under twenty years of age, and 26 per cent was over fifty.

6. The average annual per capita income in the Boston metropolitan area was U.S.$2,650 in 1960. Approximately 10 per cent had personal incomes under $1,000, while approximately 45 per cent of the Boston population had per capita incomes of over $3,000 per annum. Twenty-five per cent of the Boston City population (26 per cent of the metropolitan area in 1960) are reported to be below the official U.S. poverty line of U.S.$1,250 per capita per annum in 1968. A very high proportion of the Boston poor are from the Afro-American and Puerto Rican minorities. These have few opportunities for upward social mobility in comparison with the other ethnic groups forming the "white" majority.

7. Twenty-five per cent of the city population was classified as "poor" in 1968; this sector is unable to afford the market prices of housing at acceptable standards. Below-market-price housing in the city is provided mainly by the Boston Housing Authority's 35 projects (with a total of 14,488 units in 1967). In 1965, two other programs were initiated with state and federal aid (leased public housing and 221.d.3 government housing program). Rents for two-bedroom BHA apartments were approximately U.S.$60 and for the 221.d.3, U.S.$100. Families with incomes under $3,600 per annum can scarcely afford the cheaper BHA housing which in any case is in short supply; in 1967, the demand exceeded vacancies by 250 per cent. At that time no projects had been built since 1954. The 10 to 15 per cent in the lowest income sector are obliged to rent a rapidly decreasing stock of slum tenements. (At least 15,000 housing units, mostly in low-income areas, will have been demolished for highway and renewal developments between 1960 and 1970.)

BOSTON   42° 20'N

WIND

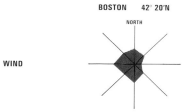

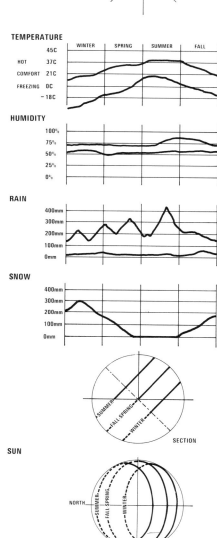

TEMPERATURE

	WINTER	SPRING	SUMMER	FALL
	45C			
HOT	37C			
COMFORT	21C			
FREEZING	0C			
	−18C			

HUMIDITY

100%
75%
50%
25%
0%

RAIN

400mm
300mm
200mm
100mm
0mm

SNOW

400mm
300mm
200mm
100mm
0mm

SUN

SECTION

NORTH

PLAN

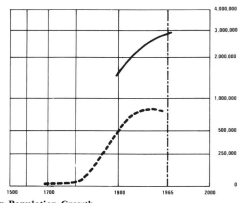

Urban Population Growth
urban area: solid line; city proper: broken line
horizontal: dates; vertical: population

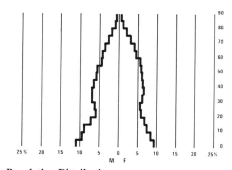

Urban Population Distribution
Census, 1959; population, 2,589,300
males: M. 1,243,163; females: F. 1,346,138
horizontal: percentages; vertical: ages

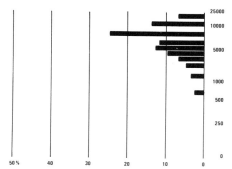

Urban Annual Income Distribution
Census, 1959; households, 640,526
horizontal: percentages; vertical: dollars

UTILITIES		SERVICES	
WATER		SCHOOLS	
SEWAGE		HEALTH	
ELECTRICITY		REFUSE COLLECTION	
PAVED ROADS		PUBLIC TRANSPORT	
TELEPHONE		RECREATION	
		FIRE	
		POLICE	

The chart illustrates the approximate availability of utilities and services at four levels: no provision at all, very limited or occasional, generally available but inadequate, and adequate or normal service.
Quality of information: Approximate

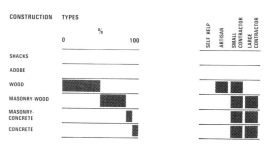

CONSTRUCTION TYPES

SHACKS
ADOBE
WOOD
MASONRY-WOOD
MASONRY-CONCRETE
CONCRETE

SELF HELP / ARTISAN / SMALL CONTRACTOR / LARGE CONTRACTOR

The chart shows (1) approximate percentage of each construction type within the total number of dwellings and (2) building group that generally produces each type.
Quality of information: Approximate

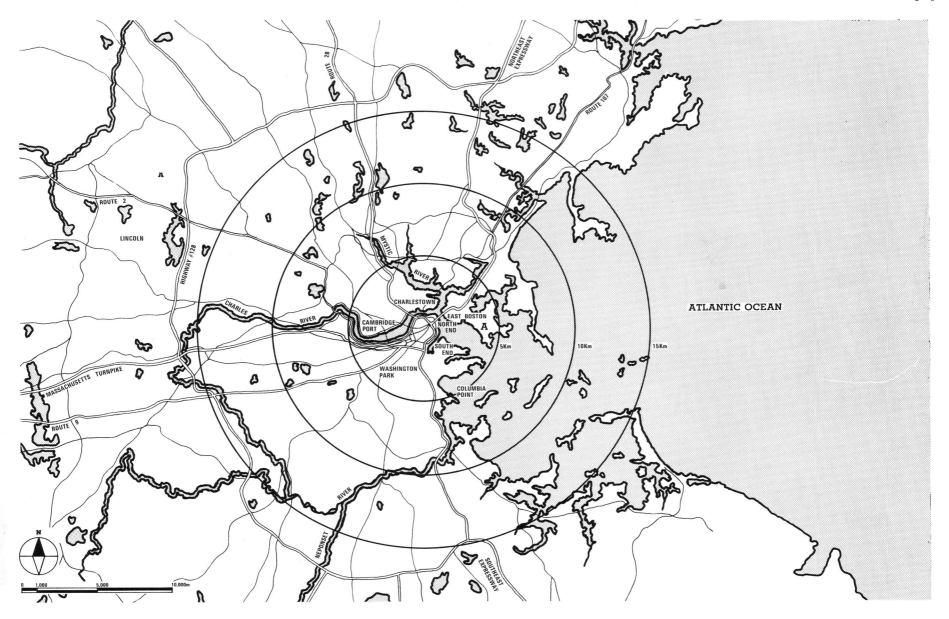

URBAN AREA, BOSTON, Massachusetts, U.S.A.
TOPOGRAPHY AND CIRCULATION
Sources: Gulf Oil Corporation Map, 1966
Quality of information: Approximate

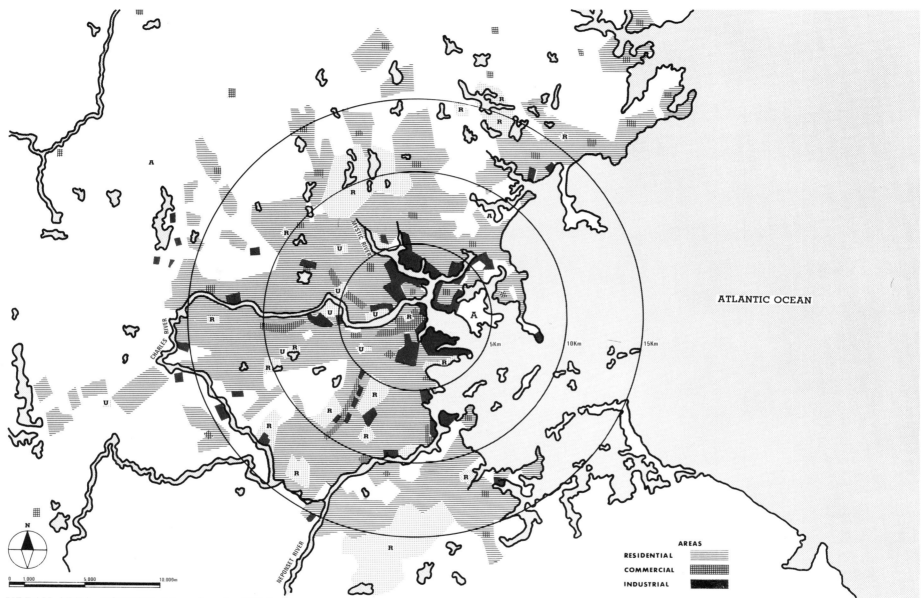

ATLANTIC OCEAN

5Km   10Km   15Km

CHARLES RIVER

MYSTIC RIVER

NEPONSET RIVER

N

0   1,000   5,000   10,000m

AREAS

RESIDENTIAL

COMMERCIAL

INDUSTRIAL

URBAN AREA, BOSTON, Massachusetts, U.S.A.
LAND-USE PATTERN
Sources: Estimate, D. Brown, 1967
Quality of information: Tentative
R: RECREATION; **A**: AIRPORT; **U**: UNIVERSITY

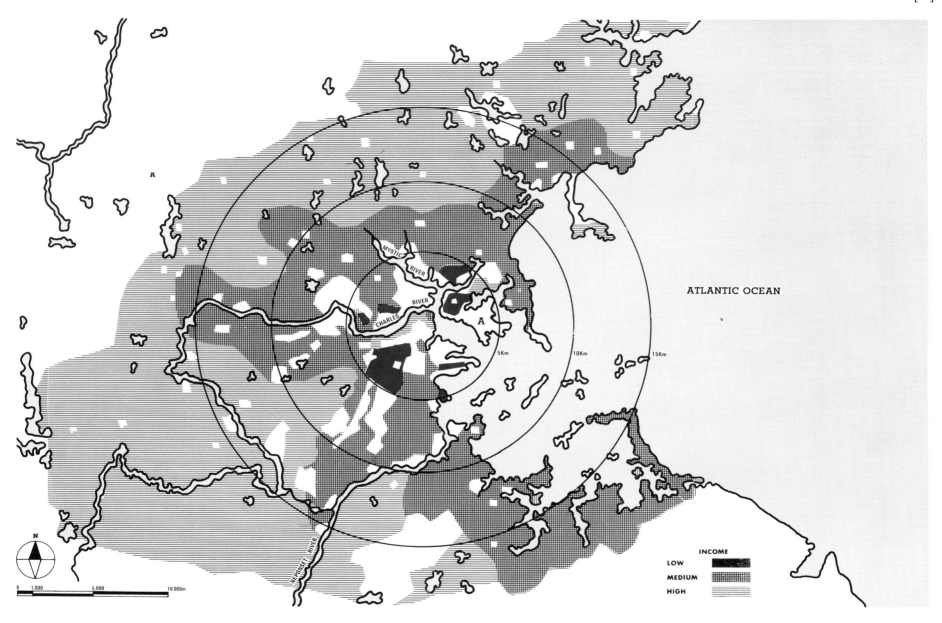

ATLANTIC OCEAN

MYSTIC RIVER

CHARLES RIVER

NEPONSET RIVER

5Km   10Km   15Km

INCOME
LOW
MEDIUM
HIGH

N

0   1,000   5,000   10,000m

URBAN AREA, BOSTON, Massachusetts, U.S.A.
INCOME PATTERN
Sources: Estimate, F. Smith, 1967
Quality of information: Tentative

LIMA, Peru

1. Lima is located on an irrigated, alluvial plain between the arid foothills of the Andes and the Pacific Ocean, latitude 12° South, longitude 77° West; although there is no rainfall, humidity is extremely high, and the area is covered by low clouds from April to November; high winds are unknown, and the temperature range is slight, although its effects are increased by the humidity.

2. Founded by Pizarro in 1535 during the conquest of Tahuantinsuyo, the Inca Empire, Lima was Vice-regal capital of the South American Spanish colonies through the sixteenth century and one of four administrative divisions in the eighteenth century. Capital of Peru shortly after Independence in 1821, Lima and its adjacent port of Callao have maintained their pre-eminence as the center of trade and, in the twentieth century, of industrial development.

3. In 1967 the annual per capita income of the metropolitan area was estimated at U.S.$350, three times that of the rest of Peru and representing 42.5 per cent of the GNP.

4. Lima is the seat of a higly centralized national government, elected by all literate, adult persons. Local elections were reintroduced in 1965 for municipal governments; the metropolitan area is divided into 25 municipalities whose authority over urban development is limited to the issue of building licenses and inspections. Authorization for subdivisions are made by the national planning agencies.

5. The estimated population of Lima in 1968 is 2,800,000 assuming a 5.5 per cent average annual increase since 1961; approximately half the increase is due to immigration from provincial areas; 50 per cent of the metropolitan population is under twenty years of age.

6. There are no major ethnic or cultural divisions that are not tied to the income class structure; the great majority of the 0.3 per cent of households with

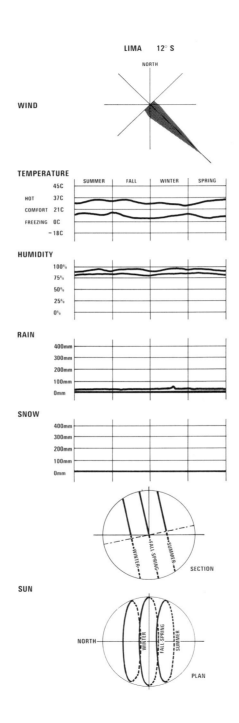

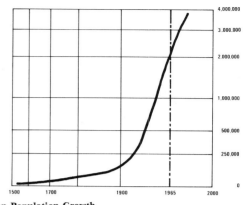

Urban Population Growth
horizontal: dates; vertical: population

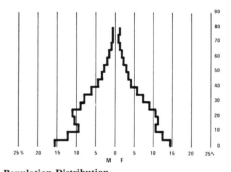

Urban Population Distribution
Census, 1961; population, 1,845,900
males: M. ———; females: F. ———
horizontal: percentages; vertical: ages

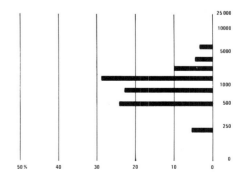

Urban Annual Income Distribution
J.N.V. data 1964; households, 331,000
horizontal: percentages; vertical: dollars

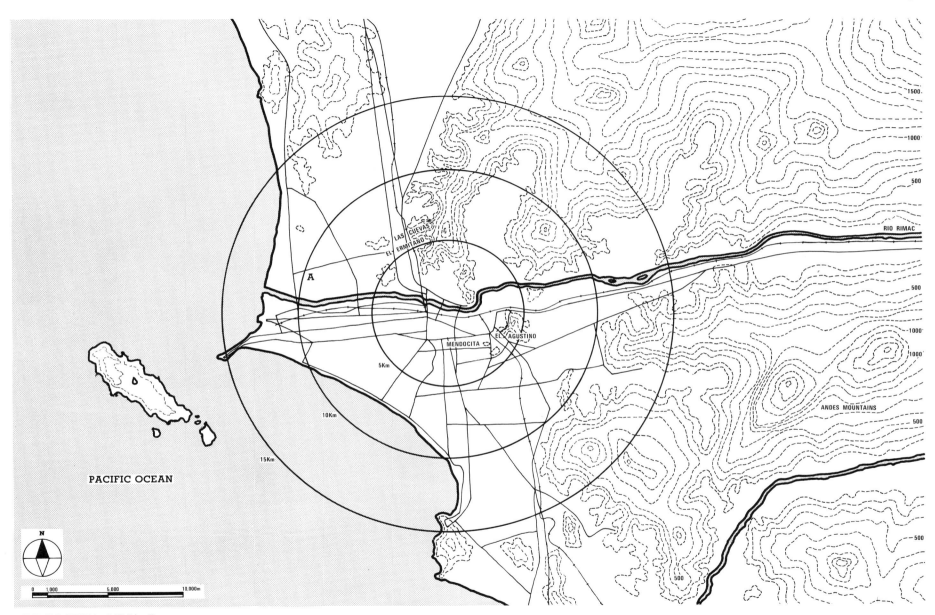

URBAN AREA, LIMA, Peru
TOPOGRAPHY AND CIRCULATION
Sources: Planos de los Municipios Distritales de Lima y
        Alrededores, 1965
Quality of information: Accurate

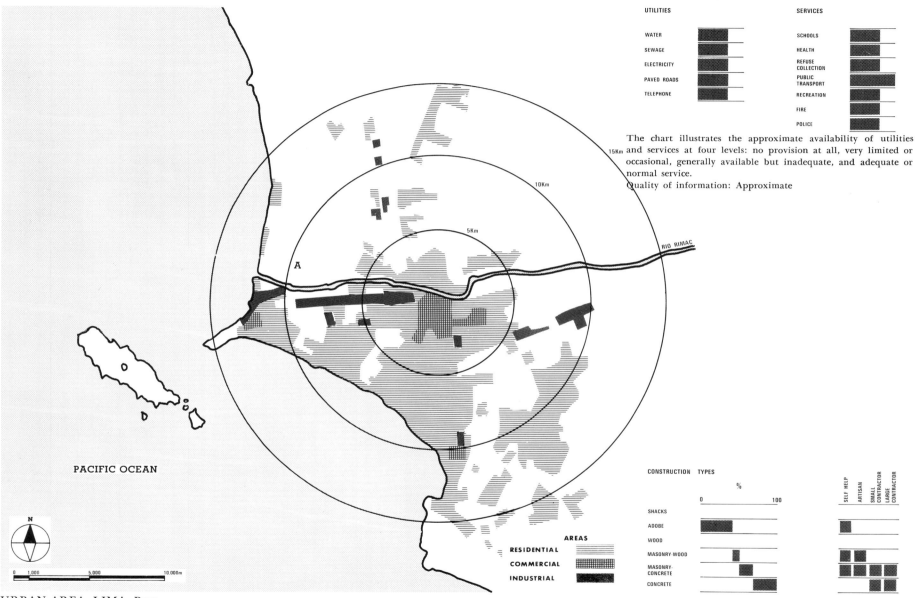

UTILITIES

WATER
SEWAGE
ELECTRICITY
PAVED ROADS
TELEPHONE

SERVICES

SCHOOLS
HEALTH
REFUSE COLLECTION
PUBLIC TRANSPORT
RECREATION
FIRE
POLICE

The chart illustrates the approximate availability of utilities and services at four levels: no provision at all, very limited or occasional, generally available but inadequate, and adequate or normal service.
Quality of information: Approximate

15Km
10Km
5Km
RIO RIMAC
A

PACIFIC OCEAN

AREAS
RESIDENTIAL
COMMERCIAL
INDUSTRIAL

N

0 1,000   5,000   10,000m

URBAN AREA, LIMA, Peru
LAND-USE PATTERN
Sources: Planos de los Municipios Distritales de Lima y
        Alrededores, 1965
Quality of information: Approximate

CONSTRUCTION TYPES
%
0   100

SELF HELP
ARTISAN
SMALL CONTRACTOR
LARGE CONTRACTOR

SHACKS
ADOBE
WOOD
MASONRY-WOOD
MASONRY-CONCRETE
CONCRETE

The chart shows (1) approximate percentage of each construction type within the total number of dwellings and (2) building group that generally produces each type.
Quality of information: Approximate

incomes more than U.S.$8,000 are European types; the vast majority of those of predominantly Andean Indian origin, together with the Negro minority, are in the lower income sectors. There is a substantial degree of socioeconomic mobility between the lowest income level (around U.S.$300 per annum) and the skilled wage level (around U.S.$1500 p.a.) which includes approximately 80 per cent of the metropolitan population.

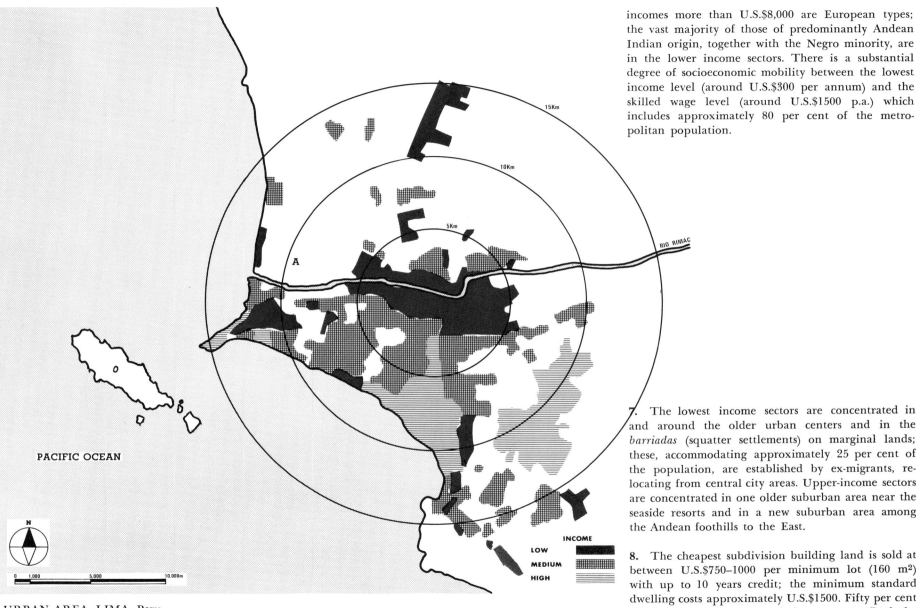

7. The lowest income sectors are concentrated in and around the older urban centers and in the *barriadas* (squatter settlements) on marginal lands; these, accommodating approximately 25 per cent of the population, are established by ex-migrants, relocating from central city areas. Upper-income sectors are concentrated in one older suburban area near the seaside resorts and in a new suburban area among the Andean foothills to the East.

8. The cheapest subdivision building land is sold at between U.S.$750–1000 per minimum lot (160 m²) with up to 10 years credit; the minimum standard dwelling costs approximately U.S.$1500. Fifty per cent of the metropolitan population cannot afford the commercial costs owing to high interest rates (minimum 9 per cent through nonprofit savings and loan associations).

PACIFIC OCEAN

INCOME
LOW
MEDIUM
HIGH

N

0   1,000   5,000   10,000m

URBAN AREA, LIMA, Peru
INCOME PATTERN
Sources: Planos de los Municipios Distritales de Lima y
          Alrededores, 1965
Quality of information: Approximate

A: AIRPORT

15Km
10Km
5Km
RIO RIMAC
A

AREQUIPA, Peru

1. Arequipa, the second city of Peru, is situated near the confluence of two small rivers, one of which is seasonal, that irrigate small but intensively cultivated areas in the desert region between the Andean Cordillera of southern Peru and the Pacific Ocean, latitude 16° South, longitude 72° West. At an altitude of 2,200 meters the city has an extremely dry climate, subject to a very short rainy season in January and with marked temperature changes between day and night. Earthquakes are common, and the city has been very badly damaged several times during its history.

2. Founded by Pizarro in 1540, Arequipa served as a staging post on the route between the seacoast (100 kms to the west) and the Titicaca plateau (200 kms to the east) and as a centre of secular and religious administration. It is the Departmental Capital and the urban and industrial center of the region defined by the railway linking Cuzco and the Titicaca (Puno) basin with the sea (at Mollendo-Matarani); this region was modified by the connection of Arequipa with the national highway network in 1954.

3. In 1961 the annual per capita income of the Department of Arequipa (50 per cent of which resides in the city or near it) was U.S.$210. The economy is not growing significantly.

4. Arequipa is the capital of one of 21 Departments, in which the highest authority, the Prefecture, is appointed by the central government. It is the headquarters of a regional development board that controls a significant proportion of the public works and housing built in the Department and in the city, and whose budget is provided by special import duties. The municipality has authority over the greater part of the built-up area (not including Miraflores where Mariano Melgar is located). Planning and building controls are exercised by the municipality through a local branch of the National Urban Planning Office which channels central-government decisions on new subdivisions; the Municipality also controls building design and construction through regulation and licensing.

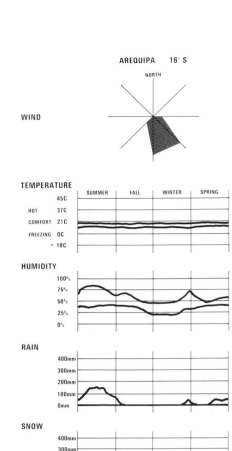

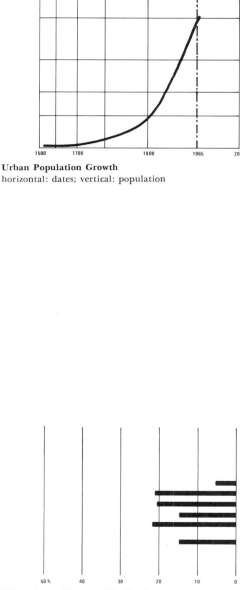

Urban Population Growth
horizontal: dates; vertical: population

Urban Annual Income Distribution
J.N.V. data, 1964; households, 31,165
horizontal: percentages; vertical: dollars

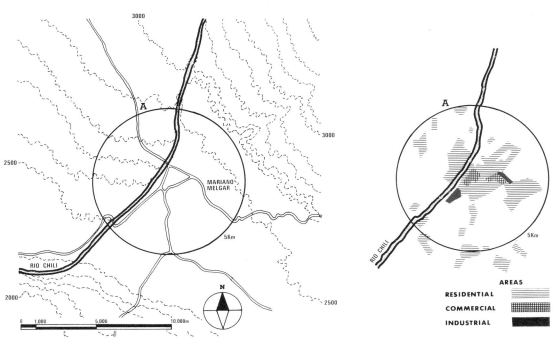

TOPOGRAPHY AND CIRCULATION
URBAN AREA, AREQUIPA, Peru

Sources: Study, Arequipa, John F. C. Turner, 1959
Quality of information: Approximate

5. The estimated population of Arequipa in 1968 is 197,500, assuming an average annual increase of 3 per cent since 1961. Approximately 0.5 per cent of the increase is due to immigration (mainly from Cuzco and the Titicaca basin).

6. To an even more marked degree than in Lima, there is a close correlation between socioeconomic status and the proportion of Peruvian Indian blood (there are very few Negroes or Asians in the area). Fifty-four per cent of urban households receive annual incomes of less than U.S.$720; 40 per cent receive incomes between U.S.$720 and U.S.$2,000; 5 1/2 per cent between U.S.$2,000 and U.S.$3,000, and less than one per cent receive incomes of over U.S.$3,000 (still below the "poverty line" in the U.S.A.).

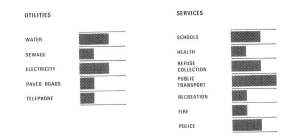

LAND-USE PATTERN
A: AIRPORT

The chart illustrates the approximate availability of utilities and services at four levels: no provision at all, very limited or occasional, generally available but inadequate, and adequate or normal service.

Quality of information: Approximate

7. (Up to 1960) The poorest inhabitants lived in rented rooms around the inner core of the city; a rapidly growing proportion of the wage-earning and low-salaried masses were moving out from the slums to "popular urbanizations" or squatter settlements

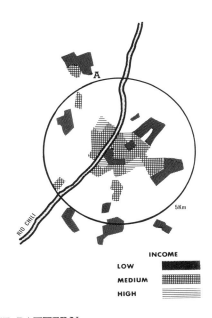

INCOME PATTERN

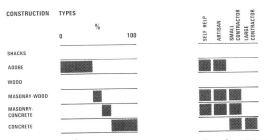

The chart shows (1) approximate percentage of each construction type within the total number of dwellings and (2) building group that generally produces each type.

Quality of information: Approximate

of low density occupying extensive areas of state-owned desert land around the city. The numerically small upper-income sector occupied four separate developments, to the north, south, east and west of the central areas.

CIUDAD GUAYANA, Venezuela

1. Ciudad Guayana is situated at the confluence of the navigable Orinoco and the high, hydroelectric potential Caroní, 250 kilometers inland from the eastern extreme of the Venezuelan coast, latitude 8° North, longitude 63° West. At an average altitude of 50 meters, the land surface is rolling savanna with poor laterite soils and a thin cover. The climate is tropical, but rainfall, although very heavy at times, is rarely continuous.

2. The development area of Ciudad Guayana (officially named Santo Tomé de Guayana when founded in 1961) incorporates the Spanish colonial town of San Félix and the twentieth-century mining company town of Puerto Ordaz. The modern city began in 1940, with the discovery and exploitation of one of the world's highest concentrations of iron ore (Cerro Bolívar). In 1960, the Corporación Venezolana de Guayana was formed by the government to develop the well-endowed but virtually unexploited and uninhabited region, planned, with the collaboration of the Joint Center for Urban Studies of M.I.T. and Harvard University, as a "growth pole" to decentralize the heavy investment in the Caracas-Valencia area as well as to open up the region and its resources.

3. In 1965, the annual per capita income of the urban area was approximately U.S.$770; industrial investment between 1961 and 1965 had grown at an average rate of 33 per cent per annum.

4. There are two principal authorities—the Corporación, which controls all but an insignificant proportion of investment in industry and infrastructure, and the Municipality, with its seat in the original township of San Félix, the representative and legislative organ of the local population. The latter has had no control and little influence over city development and planning decisions that were taken in the Corporación's central offices in Caracas.

5. The population in May 1967 was 96,400. Between 1960 and 1967 the average annual increase was 11

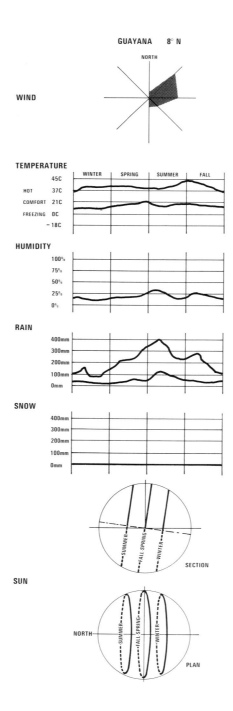

GUAYANA   8° N

WIND

TEMPERATURE

HUMIDITY

RAIN

SNOW

SUN

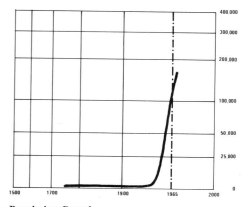

Urban Population Growth
horizontal: dates; vertical: population

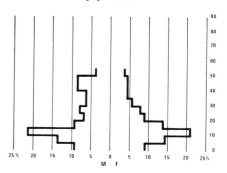

Urban Population Distribution
C.S.E.D. Census, 1967; population 96,373
males: M. 47,640; females: F. 48,733
horizontal: percentages; vertical: ages

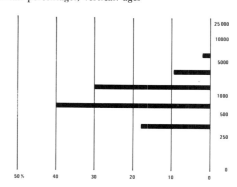

Urban Annual Income Distribution
Census, 1965
horizontal: percentages; vertical: dollars

per cent, two thirds of which was accounted for by immigration from all parts of Venezuela. Approximately 55 per cent of the population are under twenty years of age and only 4 per cent are over fifty. The great majority of households are young, nuclear families.

6. Two per cent of the population receive annual household incomes of over U.S.$4,500, and most of these are temporarily resident technical, professional, or managerial personnel from Caracas or foreign countries (principally the United States). A substantial proportion, 18 per cent, have incomes of less than U.S.$500, the minimum necessary for the average family to maintain themselves in good health. There is a small "middle class"—about 10 per cent have incomes of between U.S.$2,500 and U.S.$4,500. There is a high degree of socioeconomic mobility from the lowest levels (barring incomplete and otherwise handicapped families) to the skilled annual wage level of around U.S.$2,000. There are fewer ethnic contrasts in Venezuela (excepting the substantial negro minority), and it is, in any case, a less "class conscious" society than either Peru or Colombia.

7. Residential settlement is highly differentiated by socioeconomic sector. With the few exceptions of original families of San Félix, the upper-income group live in the Puerto Ordaz, on the west bank of the River Caroní, the area originally settled by the Orinoco Mining Company in 1940. Those with the lowest incomes are concentrated in one area of Puerto Ordaz, on the river bank at the ferry landing—the only land communication with San Félix before 1966, when the present bridge was opened; the lowest income sectors on the east bank are scattered throughout the area but tend to concentrate along the road between San Felix and the ferry site and bridge and, also, on the eastern fringe of San Félix.

8. The CVG has initiated several projects for land, community facilities and credit assistance for self-help housing (with posterior installation of utilities); the majority of the population are unable to afford the costs or are otherwise ineligible; squatting is widespread (over 40 per cent in 1966).

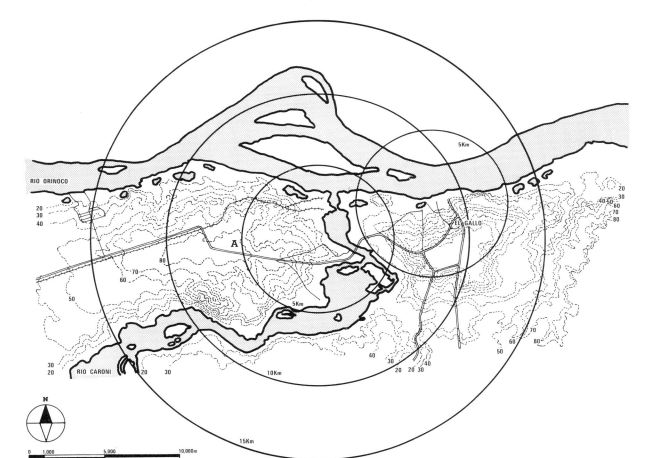

URBAN AREA, CIUDAD GUAYANA, Venezuela
TOPOGRAPHY AND CIRCULATION
Sources: Corporación Venezolana de Guayana Site Plan
Quality of information: Accurate

The chart illustrates the approximate availability of utilities and services at four levels: no provision at all, very limited or occasional, generally available but inadequate, and adequate or normal service.

Quality of information: Approximate

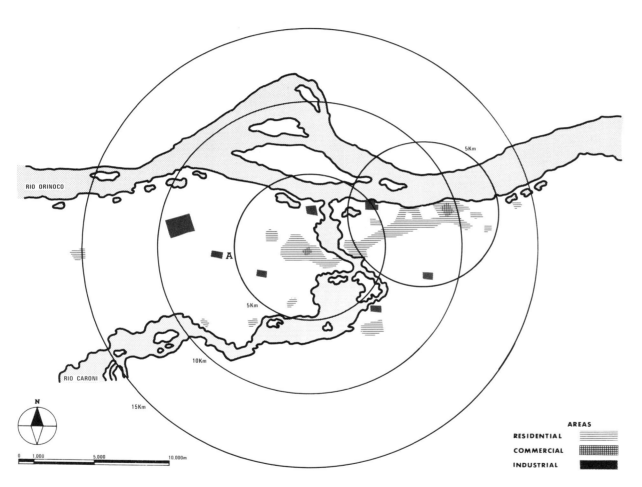

URBAN AREA, CIUDAD GUAYANA, Venezuela
LAND-USE PATTERN
Sources: Corporación Venezolana de Guayana Site Plan
Quality of information: Approximate

A: AIRPORT

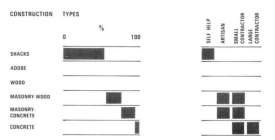

The chart shows (1) approximate percentage of each construction type within the total number of dwellings and (2) building group that generally produces each type.

Quality of information: Approximate

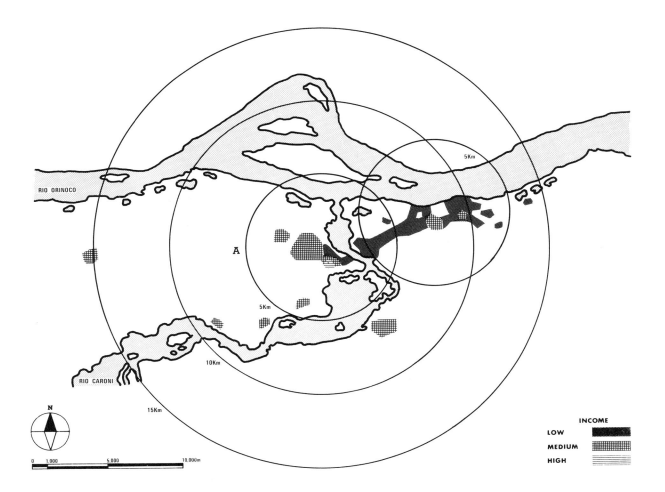

RIO ORINOCO

5Km

A

5Km

10Km

RIO CARONI

15Km

N

0   1,000   5,000   10,000m

INCOME

LOW

MEDIUM

HIGH

URBAN AREA, CIUDAD GUAYANA, Venezuela
LAND-USE PATTERN
Sources: Corporación Venezolana de Guayana Site Plan
Quality of information: Approximate

MEDELLIN, Colombia

1. Medellín is situated in an interandine valley in the western part of Colombia at an altitude of 1400 meters; latitude 6° North, 76° West. The climate is mild and subtropical with year-round but rarely continuous rainfall with a relatively dry season between December and March.

2. Medellín was founded in 1616 but did not become the capital of the Department of Antioquía until 1826. After 1940, the city became an important industrial center, competing for a time with Bogotá, the national capital.

3. The gross industrial produce per capita for 1960 was U.S.$580. Between 1951 and 1964 there was little change in the proportion of industrial workers (19 to 20 per cent), so that it appears that industrial growth has been at approximately the same rate as the urban population growth (that is, between 5 and 6 per cent per annum).

4. The Municipality of Medellín is divided into six *comunas* or districts; the principal departments of government are administered by the Municipality with a total expenditure of approximately U.S. $11,000,000 in 1962 (that is, U.S.$16 per capita). Planning controls are exercised by the Municipal Planning Office; Medellín is one of the few cities (with transitional economies) to administer a property-valorization policy, and this contributes substantially to the public works program.

5. The estimated population of Medellín in 1968 is 983,000—a 27 per cent increase over the population at the time of the 1964 census (773,000)—an annual growth rate of just over 6 per cent. In 1964, 54 per cent of the population was under twenty years of age.

6. Ethnically, the population is relatively homogenous (only in the tropical, coastal cities are there high proportions of Negroes); the indigenous pre-Colombian population was never large, and only among the lower-income sectors are traces clearly evident. In 1964, 23 per cent of the urban population had

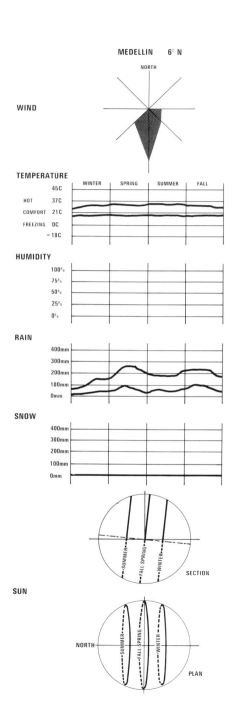

MEDELLIN   6° N

WIND

TEMPERATURE

HUMIDITY

RAIN

SNOW

SUN

SECTION

PLAN

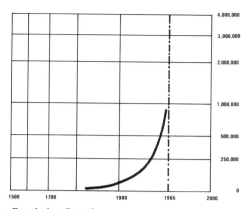

Urban Population Growth
horizontal: dates; vertical: population

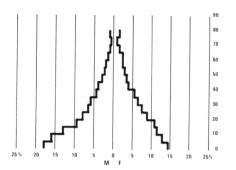

Urban Population Distribution
Census, 1964; population, 772,900
males: M. ———; females: F. ———
horizontal: dates; vertical: ages

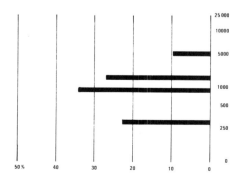

Urban Annual Income Distribution
Estimated 1966; population, 830,000
horizontal: percentages; vertical: dollars

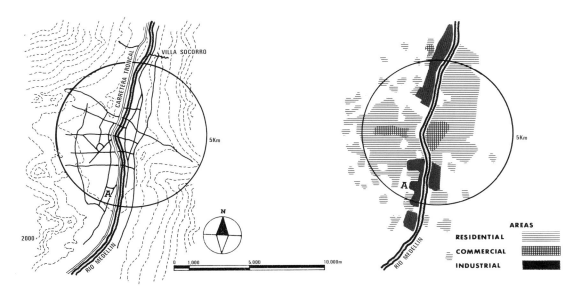

TOPOGRAPHY AND CIRCULATION

URBAN AREA, MEDELLIN, Colombia
Sources: Master Plan—Medellín, 1963
Quality of information: Approximate

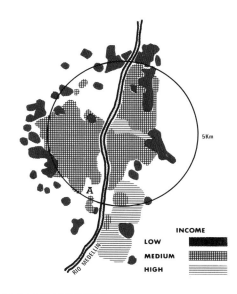

LAND-USE PATTERN

A: AIRPORT

INCOME PATTERN

annual incomes of less than U.S.$864 and 10 per cent had incomes of over U.S.$3360. One third had incomes between U.S.$864 and U.S.$1632. Most semi-skilled to skilled wages (in 1962) ranged between a minimum of U.S.$45 to U.S.$90 per month, i.e., between U.S.$540 and U.S.$1080 per annum.

7. The areas with the highest concentrations of low-income households is the southern quadrant of the inner ring (adjacent to the Central Business District) and the periphery in which the *barrios piratas* (clandestine subdivisions) are located. Most of these, which were reported to accommodate 15.5 per cent of the population in 1965, are on land above the contour for gravity-distributed water supply, and almost all are on rugged terrain. The upper-income sector is distributed between two areas, in the northeastern quadrant of the inner ring and in a suburban area to the southwest.

8. In the *barrios piratas* low-income families can obtain plots for the equivalent of between four and six

The chart illustrates the approximate availability of utilities and services at four levels: no provision at all, very limited or occasional, generally available but inadequate, and adequate or normal service.

Quality of information: Approximate

average monthly incomes (approximately U.S.$275 in 1964), and as credit is offered by the clandestine vendors, many low-income families are able to settle and build their own homes cheaply (that is, by stages and without regard to official regulations and without having to pay for utilities, as these are generally non-existent). Approximately 10,000 low-cost units were

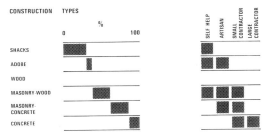

The chart shows (1) approximate percentage of each construction type within the total number of dwellings and (2) building group that generally produces each type.

Quality of information: Approximate

built by the government (the Instituto de Crédito Territorial) between 1962 and 1965. (The quantitative deficit in 1964 for urban housing throughout Colombia was calculated to be 310,000 units, 30,000 more than in 1962; Medellín represented approximately 9 per cent of the urban population in 1964 so that the local deficit would have been around 28,000 units in 1964–1965.)

2. LOCALITIES

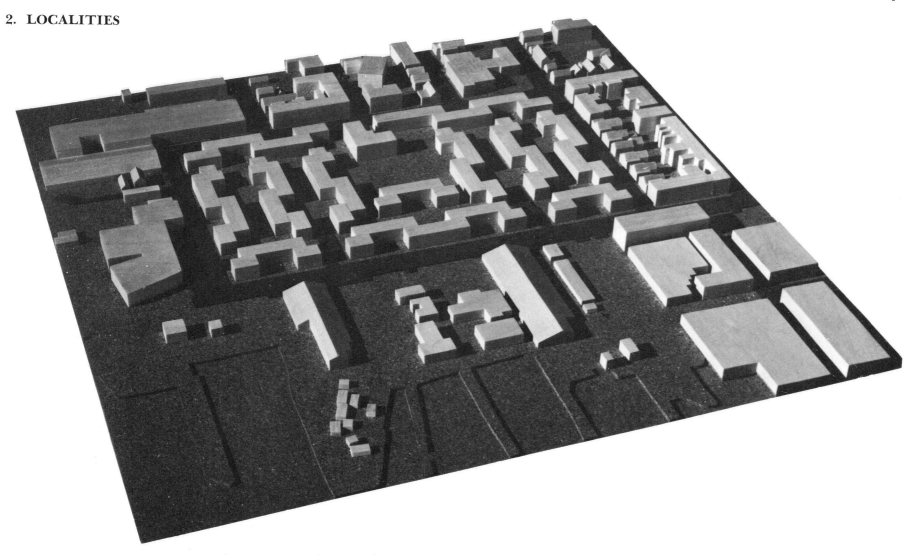

EAST BOSTON, Boston, Massachusetts, U.S.A.

Location: East Boston is situated about two kilometers from the central business district. It is bounded on the north, west, and south by deep-water port facilities of Boston Harbor and on the east by Logan International Airport. East Boston is separated from the city proper by this water barrier, but it has direct rapid access via automobile and rapid-transit tunnels. East Boston is one of the areas of Boston more readily accessible to the central business district.

Origins: By 1840, East Boston was one of several peripheral manufacturing areas within a few minutes of the inner city. In the twentieth century the area has declined, as most of the available industrial land in the area is along water fronts and therefore suited only to a limited and declining number of specialized uses. The development of the (still expanding) international airport in the 1940's has not yet led to the establishment of new associated industries.

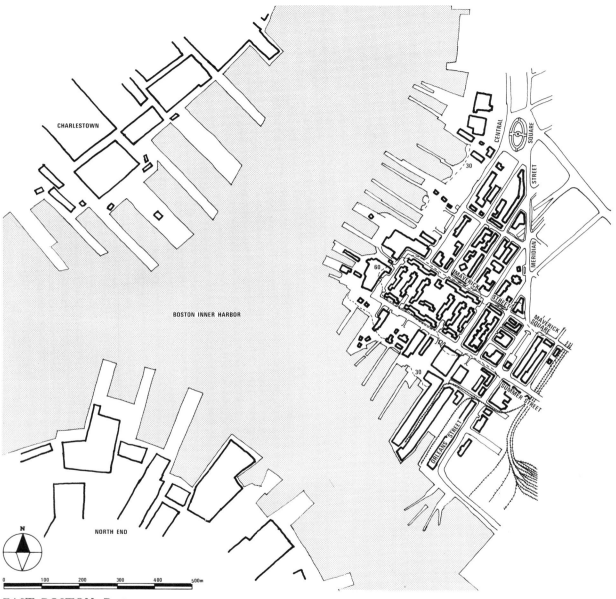

CHARLESTOWN

BOSTON INNER HARBOR

30

60

MAVERICK STREET

CENTRAL SQUARE

MERIDIAN STREET

MAVERICK SQUARE

SUMMER STREET

30

ORLEANS STREET

NORTH END

N

0   100   200   300   400   500m

EAST BOSTON, Boston
LOCALITY PLAN
Sources: City of Boston, Topographic and Planimetric Survey,
      B.R.A., 1962
Quality of information: Accurate

Layout: Built mainly on filled marshland, East Boston was set out on the standard rectangular block-grid plan, with the industrial areas situated on the water fronts.

Population: The residential population of East Boston is declining: between 1950 and 1960, the population dropped by 20 per cent. No other data is available.

EAST BOSTON, Boston Air view of the peninsula with Logan International Airport. The case-study area is in the lower right corner. (1966) (*opposite page*)

Land Use: The entire area is heavily built up, and there is no room for residential expansion; a relatively high proportion of the area is occupied by industry or vacant industrial land and buildings which bear the same relationship to the locality as Charlestown to the North End.

Incomes: The 1959 census showed an average annual household income of U.S.$6,100, slightly below the average for the metropolitan area; a relatively small proportion had very low incomes, however— only 7 per cent had household incomes of under U.S.$2,000, (as against 14, 17, and 41 per cent in the North End, Columbia Point, and the South End respectively).

CHARLESTOWN

CENTRAL SQUARE

SS

R

MERIDIAN STREET

Pk

MAVERICK STREET

S

PO

S

H

S

S

R

F

P

SUMMER STREET

R

MAVERICK SQUARE

BOSTON INNER HARBOR

ORLEANS STREET

NORTH END

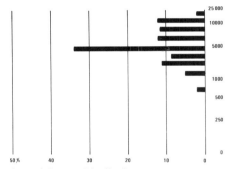

Locality Annual Income Distribution
Census, 1960; tract E-3; households, 196
horizontal: percentages; vertical: dollars

N

0 100 200 300 400 500m

EAST BOSTON, Boston
LOCALITY LAND-USE PATTERN
Sources: Survey, D. Brown, 1967
Quality of information: Approximate

AREAS
RESIDENTIAL
COMMERCIAL
INDUSTRIAL

H	Health	Bus (solid line)
PO	Post Office	Rapid Transit
SS	Social Services	(broken line)

Pk	Parking	Ch	Church
P	Police	R	Recreation
F	Fire Department	L	Library
S	School	U	University

EAST BOSTON, Boston Street corners on Central Square; pharmacy, restaurant. See locality plan. (1968)

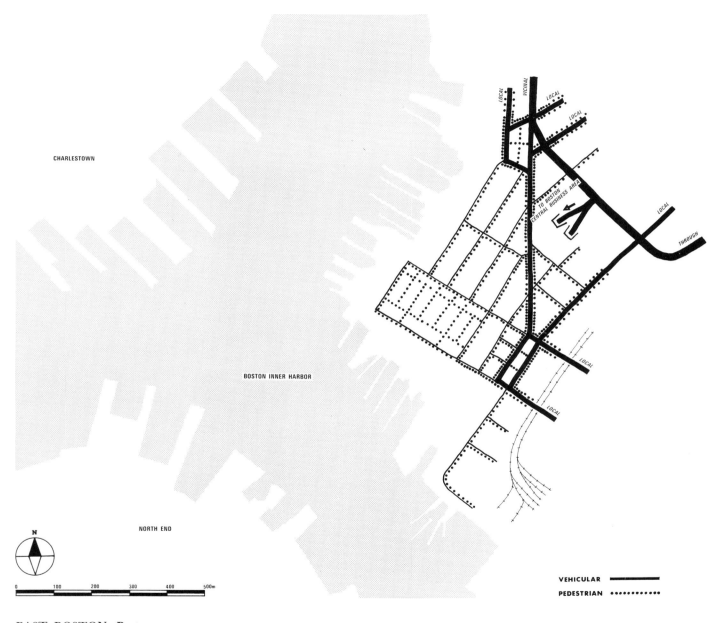

CHARLESTOWN

BOSTON INNER HARBOR

NORTH END

N

| 0 | 100 | 200 | 300 | 400 | 500m |

VEHICULAR ━━━━━━
PEDESTRIAN ●●●●●●●●●●●

EAST BOSTON, Boston
LOCALITY CIRCULATION PATTERN
Source: Estimate, D. Brown, 1967
Quality of information: Tentative

Circulation: The locality is bounded by industrial facilities and a vicinal road that isolates it from the adjacent area. The only connection to the central business district is by means of a tunnel beneath the harbor. The circulation grid within the locality stems from the bounding vicinal road.

The chart illustrates the approximate availability of utilities and services at four levels: no provision at all, very limited or occasional, generally available but inadequate, and adequate or normal service.

Quality of information: Approximate

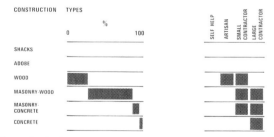

The main dwellings' construction types were grouped as follows: SHACK, ADOBE, WOOD, WOOD AND MASONRY, MASONRY AND CONCRETE, CONCRETE. The main characteristics of these types are described in the introduction.

The building industry was divided into the following groups: SELF-HELP, ARTISAN, SMALL CONTRACTOR, LARGE CONTRACTOR.

The chart shows (1) approximate percentage of each construction type within the total number of dwellings and (2) building group that generally produces each type.

Quality of information: Approximate

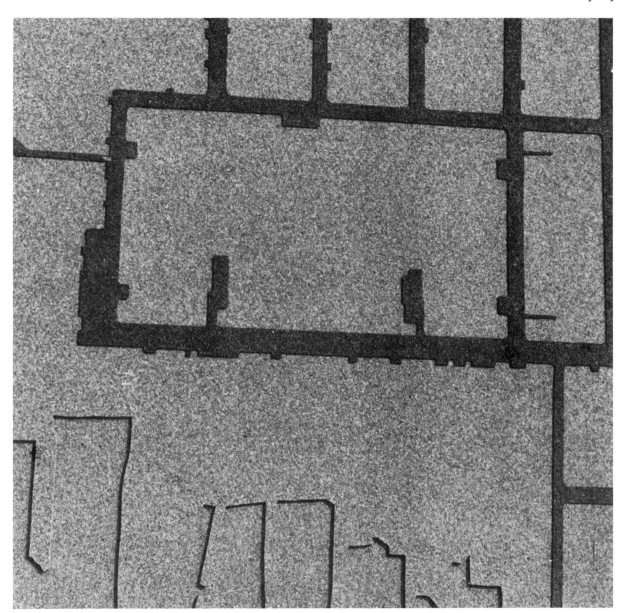

EAST BOSTON, Boston
LOCALITY SEGMENT
400 m × 400 m; scale: 1:2500
Model of raw site showing topography, main circulation layout

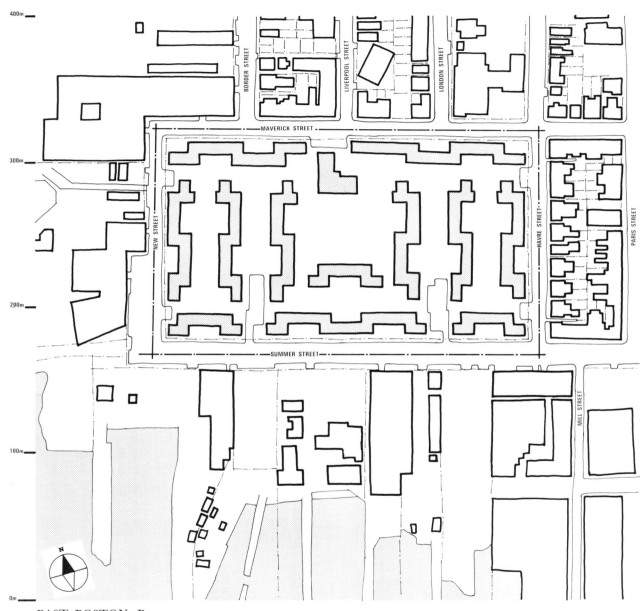

Locality Segment: The area selected for more detailed analysis is a public housing project with a land-use pattern that is distinctly different from that of the locality as a whole. Four typical 110 m × 40 m blocks were consolidated to provide the site.

LOCALITY SEGMENT

AREAS

PRIVATE OWNERSHIP	Hectares	Percentage
Dwelling Lots	2.10	13.13
Commercial	—	—
Industrial	6.10	38.13

PUBLIC OWNERSHIP		
Public Housing (Buildings)	1.30	8.12
Community Centers, Parks Playgrounds, Schools	1.95	12.19
Streets—Parking Pedestrian Walks	2.75	17.18
Water	1.80	11.25
Total	16.00	100.00

DENSITIES	Number	Hectares	N/Ha
Lots	85	16.00	5.31
Dwelling Units	666	16.00	41.63
Families	665	16.00	41.56
People (4 People/Family)	2660	16.00	166.25

Quality of information: Approximate

EAST BOSTON, Boston
LOCALITY SEGMENT PLAN
Sources: City of Boston, Topographic and Planimetric Survey,
      B.R.A., 1962; Description of public housing, Castle
      Square Relocation Program, B.R.A.

Quality of information: Accurate

SELECTED BLOCK

AREAS

PRIVATE OWNERSHIP	Hectares	Percentage
Dwelling Lots	—	—
Commercial	—	—
Industrial	—	—

PUBLIC OWNERSHIP	Hectares	Percentage
Public Housing (Buildings)	1.30	32.50
Community Center, Parks Playground, Schools	1.95	48.75
Streets—Parking Pedestrian Walks	0.75	18.75
Total	4.00	100.00

DENSITIES

	Number	Hectares	N/Ha
Lots	1	4.00	.25
Dwelling Units	414	4.00	103.50
Families	414	4.00	103.50
People (4 People/Family)	1656	4.00	414.00

CIRCULATION RATIO

$$\frac{\text{Circulation Length} = 1462 \text{ m}}{\text{Area} \quad = 4.00 \text{ Ha}} = 366 \text{ m/Ha}$$

Selected block is the area enclosed by the broken line on the Locality Segment plan.

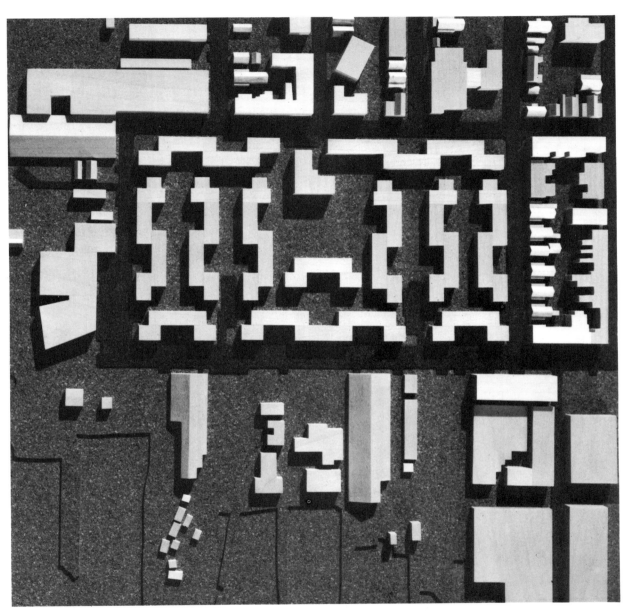

EAST BOSTON, Boston
LOCALITY SEGMENT
400 m × 400 m; scale: 1:2500
Model of developed site showing existing buildings and streets

Dwelling Group: The three-story walk-up apartment blocks contain 24 apartments, mainly of the one- and two-bedroom types. The open space, within the perimeter of the surrounding streets, is closed to vehicular traffic and as in the other public housing projects is largely occupied with fenced-off clothes-drying areas.

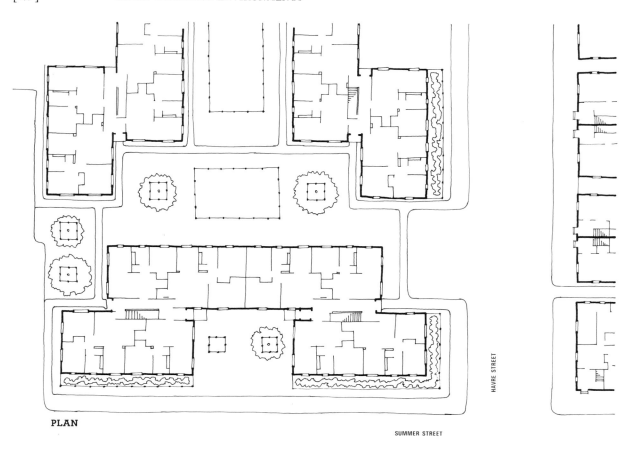

PLAN

HAVRE STREET

SUMMER STREET

SECTION

EAST BOSTON, Boston
DWELLING GROUP (Public Housing)
Sources: Project working drawings
Quality of information: Accurate

EAST BOSTON, Boston Typical wood-frame dwellings in the background; industrial yards in the foreground. (*top*)

View of the public housing shown on plans—walk-up apartments, laundry yards. (*bottom*)

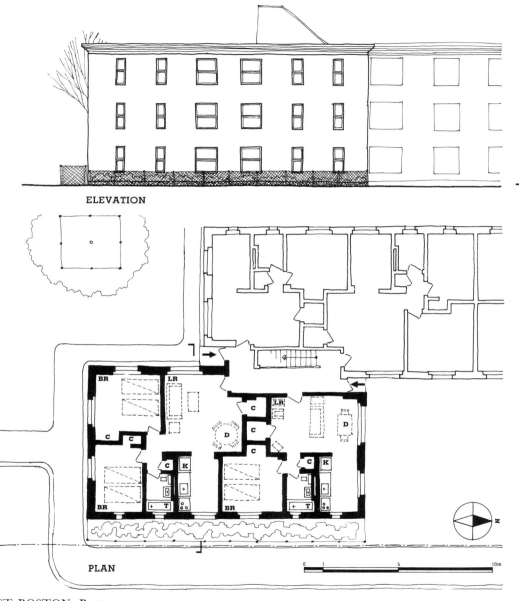

ELEVATION

SECTION

PLAN

0 1   5   10m

EAST BOSTON, Boston
TYPICAL DWELLING (Public Housing)
Sources: Project working drawings, Boston Housing Authority,
Description of public housing, Castle Square Reloca-
tion Program, B.R.A.

Quality of information: Approximate

DWELLING-UNIT AREAS

(large unit)	m^2	%
Living (BR, DR, D, LR, K, C)	41.84	64.10
Service (T, L)	4.55	6.97
Circulation	1.60	2.45
Walls	17.20	26.48
Other	—	—
Total Unit Area:	65.19	100.00

Total Lot Area: Not pertinent, public use

LR	Living Room	**K**	Kitchen
DR	Dining Room	**L**	Laundry
D	Dining	**T**	Toilet—Bathroom
BR	Bedroom	**C**	Closet

EAST BOSTON, Boston Street, neighborhood shop, children playing. The old stone pavement patched with asphalt.

EAST BOSTON, Boston

Dwelling

Design and development: Public housing (government-sponsored); instant development.
Year of construction: 1942.
Type of dwelling: Two-bedroom, walk-up apartment.
Approximate number of people per unit: 4 people.
Approximate dwelling area per person: 16.30 sq. m (large unit).
Layout: Four apartments are served by one stairway; corridors are eliminated by using rooms for circulation; no interior rooms; closets in all the rooms, including 1.20 m deep, walk-in closets; back-to-back kitchen/bathroom plumbing forms a basis for the plan.
Facilities: Kitchen; bath; basement laundry; domestic hot and cold water; central heating and electricity are provided; telephone service is available.
Components: Double-hung windows on the four exterior walls.
Type of construction: Masonry bearing walls; floors: reinforced-concrete slab.
For comparison see the following dwellings: Charlestown, Columbia Point, which are similar public housing projects in Boston.

CHARLESTOWN, Boston, Massachusetts, U.S.A.

Location: Charlestown is located across the Charles River from downtown Boston and connected by two bridges. Charlestown is also connected with the Northeast Expressway via the Mystic River Bridge.

Origins: Charlestown is the site of the first settlement in the Boston vicinity; the Massachusetts Bay Company established its first township there in 1630, naming it after King Charles I of England. The town was destroyed during the Battle of Bunker Hill in 1775, but by the end of the first decade of the nineteenth century, Charlestown had become an important shipbuilding and manufacturing center. In the middle and late decades of the century Charlestown expanded rapidly as a residential neighborhood as it was suitably situated for lower- and middle-income groups working in Boston; this trend was stimulated toward the end of the century by the timber two- and three-decker-house building boom. The locality has declined, along with East Boston, for the same reasons, the outmoding of the industrial locations and the decline of shipbuilding.

CHARLESTOWN, Boston
LOCALITY PLAN
Sources: City of Boston, Topographic and Planimetric Survey,
        B.R.A., 1962
Quality of information: Accurate

Layout: The more irregular street pattern of the oldest area was developed piecemeal around Bunker Hill in much the same way as the North End developed around Copp's Hill.

Population: The doubly asymmetrical age-sex pyramid of the locality—the heavy bias of young males and the heavy bias of older females—is due to the presence of Charlestown Naval Base and, presumably, the classic pattern of poor neighborhoods with a high proportion of fatherless families. The average age of the female population, which is unaffected by the Naval Base, is about thirty-three years, similar to the North End population.

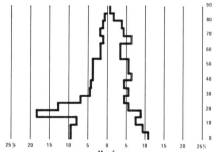

Locality Population Distribution
Census, 1960; tract C-1; population, 1907
males: M. 961; females: F. 946
horizontal: percentages; vertical: ages

CHARLESTOWN, Boston John F. Fitzgerald Expressway;
Charlestown in the background. The structural forest of the
elevated highway, the gas tanks, the billboards, and other
paraphernalia of the twentieth century surrounds the Bunker
Hill Obelisk.

LITTLE MYSTIC CANAL

R

MEDFORD STREET

S

S

R

STREET

S

MONUMEN

BUNKER HILL STREET

S

BARTLETT STREET

MYSTIC RIVER BRIDGE

S   S

BUNKER HILL
MONUMENT

R

HIGH STREET

MAIN STREET

WINTHROP
SQUARE

R

RUTHERFORD AVENUE

R

R

R

CITY
SQUARE

BOSTON INNER HARBOR

N

0   100   200   300   400   500m

AREAS

RESIDENTIAL

COMMERCIAL

INDUSTRIAL

CHARLESTOWN, Boston
LOCALITY LAND-USE PATTERN
Sources: Charlestown Urban Renewal Area Plan, B.R.A.
Quality of information: Approximate

H   Health   Bus (solid line)
PO   Post Office   Rapid Transit
SS   Social Services (broken line)

Pk   Parking   Ch   Church
P   Police   R   Recreation
F   Fire Department L   Library
S   School   U   University

Land Use: The residential and commercial area is almost entirely free of industry; the extensive industrial zone is located on filled land between the port installations. This separation is emphasized by the raised expressway and the Mystic River Bridge. Commerce, which is local, is concentrated along the two main streets connecting Charlestown with Somerville and Cambridge to the west. A rapid-transit line runs over the still appropriately named Main Street.

Incomes: The income distribution is also similar to that for the North End but with a lower center of gravity. The (1960) average household income was U.S.$5,250 per household per annum, 17 per cent below the metropolitan average but 130 per cent above the average for the South End, which is the poorest area surveyed in this series.

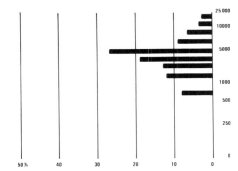

25 000
10000
5000
1000
500
250
0

50 %   40   30   20   10   0

Locality Annual Income Distribution
Census, 1960; tract C-1; households, 367
horizontal: percentages; vertical: dollars

CHARLESTOWN, Boston Elevated public transit line connecting Charlestown to Boston. Photograph is taken from the platform of City Square Station. (*opposite page*)

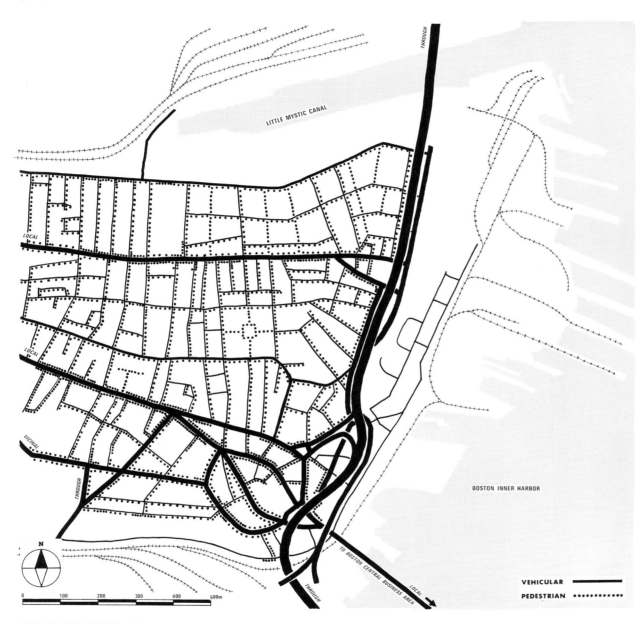

CHARLESTOWN, Boston
LOCALITY CIRCULATION PATTERN
Source: Estimate, G. Cristol, 1967
Quality of information: Tentative

Circulation: Major vehicular movement in Charlestown is generated from the industrial area and the expressway. Pedestrian movement is largely perpendicular to the main traffic streets, which also provide the public transport routes.

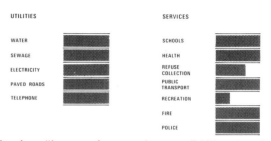

The chart illustrates the approximate availability of utilities and services at four levels: no provision at all, very limited or occasional, generally available but inadequate, and adequate or normal service.

Quality of information: Approximate

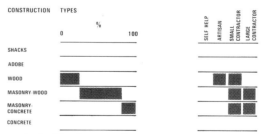

The main dwellings' construction types were grouped as follows: SHACK, ADOBE, WOOD, WOOD AND MASONRY, MASONRY AND CONCRETE, CONCRETE. The main characteristics of these types are described in the introduction.

The building industry was divided into the following groups: SELF-HELP, ARTISAN, SMALL CONTRACTOR, LARGE CONTRACTOR.

The chart shows (1) approximate percentage of each construction type within the total number of dwellings and (2) building group that generally produces each type.

Quality of information: Approximate

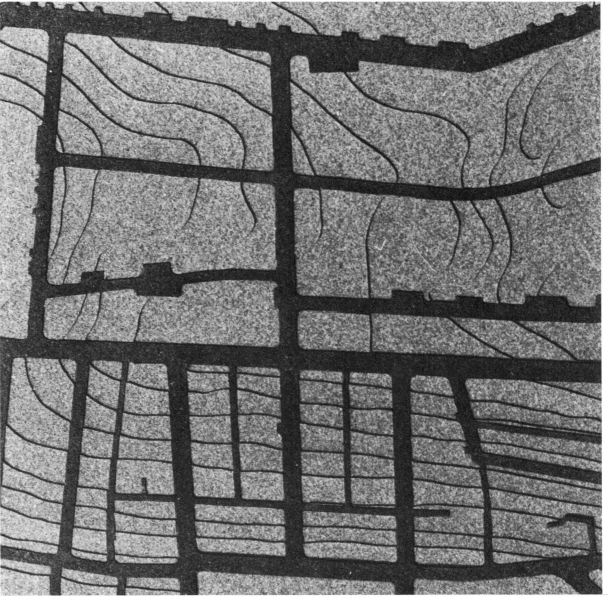

CHARLESTOWN, Boston
LOCALITY SEGMENT
400 m × 400 m; scale: 1:2500
Model of raw site showing topography, main circulation layout

CHARLESTOWN, Boston
LOCALITY SEGMENT PLAN
Sources: City of Boston, Topographic and Planimetric Survey,
        B.R.A., 1962; Description of public housing, Castle
        Square Relocation Program, B.R.A.

Quality of information: Accurate

Locality Segment: Half the area shown is occupied by a typical public housing project, the other half by typical blocks of mixed residential and commercial use. The latter are based on a system similar to that of the South End, service alleys giving double access to the plots, some of which have been subdivided.

LOCALITY SEGMENT

AREAS

PRIVATE OWNERSHIP	Hectares	Percentage
Dwelling Lots	4.50	28.13
Commercial	—	—
Industrial	1.20	7.50
PUBLIC OWNERSHIP		
Public Housing (Buildings)	1.50	9.38
Community Centers, Parks Playgrounds, Schools	3.70	23.12
Streets—Parking Pedestrian Walks	5.10	31.87
Total	16.00	100.00

DENSITIES	Number	Hectares	N/Ha
Lots	239	16.00	14.94
Dwelling Units	897	16.00	56.06
Families	897	16.00	56.06
People	3588	16.00	224.25
(3.2 People/Family)			

Quality of information: Approximate

SELECTED BLOCK

AREAS

PRIVATE OWNERSHIP	Hectares	Percentage
Dwelling Lots	—	—
Commercial	—	—
Industrial	—	—

PUBLIC OWNERSHIP		
Public Housing (Buildings)	0.45	25.00
Community Centers, Parks Playground, Schools	0.80	44.44
Streets—Parking Pedestrian Walks	0.55	30.56
Total	1.80	100.00

DENSITIES	Number	Hectares	N/Ha
Lots	1	1.80	.56
Dwelling Units	178	1.80	98.89
Families	178	1.80	98.89
People (3.2 People/Family)	712	1.80	395.56

CIRCULATION RATIO

$$\frac{\text{Circulation Length} = 700 \text{ m}}{\text{Area} \qquad = 1.80 \text{ Ha}} = 386 \text{ m/Ha}$$

Selected block is the area enclosed by the broken line on the Locality Segment plan.

CHARLESTOWN, Boston
LOCALITY SEGMENT
400 m × 400 m; scale: 1:2500
Model of developed site showing existing buildings and streets

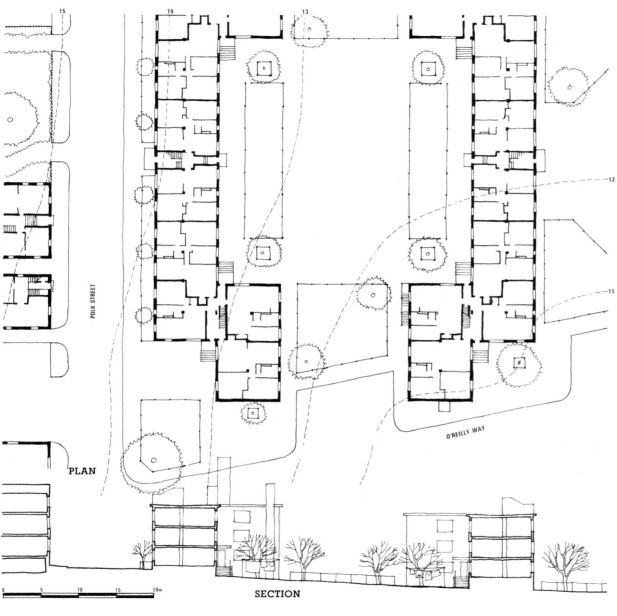

PLAN

SECTION

Dwelling Group: The public housing project is a standard type: each block consists of thirty (one-, two-, and three-bedroom) apartments on three floors. Each pair of blocks encloses an open space, parts of which are fenced off for clothes drying and to protect the trees and gardens. The remainder is asphalted. Alternating with these semiprivate areas are either vehicular streets or walkways.

CHARLESTOWN, Boston
DWELLING GROUP (Public Housing)
Sources: Project working drawings, B.H.A.
Quality of information: Accurate

CHARLESTOWN, Boston Bunker Hill Monument from a typical residential street. Compare with preceding photograph of the obelisk. (*opposite page*)

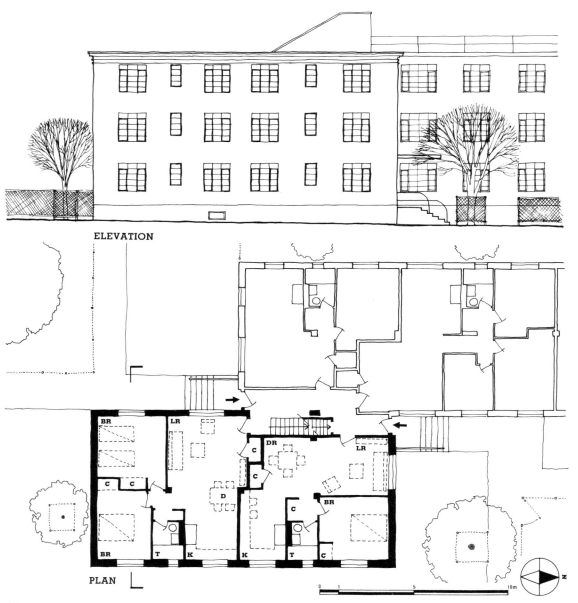

ELEVATION

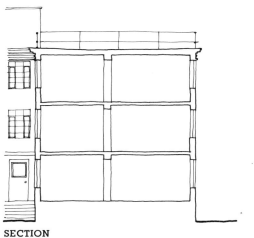

SECTION

PLAN

CHARLESTOWN, Boston
TYPICAL DWELLING (Public Housing)
Sources: Project working drawings, Boston Housing Authority,
    Description of public housing, Castle Square Reloca-
    tion Program

Quality of information: Approximate

DWELLING-UNIT AREAS

(large unit)	m^2	%
Living (BR, DR, D, LR, K, C)	50.06	72.10
Service (T, L)	5.44	7.68
Circulation	1.65	2.34
Walls	12.65	17.88
Other	—	—
Total Unit Area:	69.80	100.00

Total Lot Area: Not pertinent, public use

LR	Living Room	**K**	Kitchen
DR	Dining Room	**L**	Laundry
D	Dining	**T**	Toilet—Bathroom
BR	Bedroom	**C**	Closet

CHARLESTOWN, Boston Residential street on Baker Street. Single-family row houses. The street provides the only parking space for the dwellings.

CHARLESTOWN, Boston

Dwelling
Design and development: Public housing (government-sponsored); instant development.
Year of construction: 1940.
Type of dwelling: Two-bedroom, walk-up apartment.
Approximate number of people per unit: 4 people.
Approximate dwelling area per person: 17.54 sq. m (large unit).
Layout: Almost identical to the East Boston dwelling; four apartments served by one stairway; corridors within the apartment are eliminated by using rooms for circulation; there are no interior rooms, closets in all rooms are 0.60 m deep. Back-to-back kitchen/bathroom plumbing forms the basis for the plan.
Facilities: Kitchen; bath; basement laundry, domestic hot and cold water; central heating and electricity are provided; telephone service is available. There is a more generous kitchen counter (work space) in this apartment than in the East Boston example.
Components: Casement windows. It should be noticed that there are no windows in the south wall, which is the best orientation. This omission could be explained but not justified. In other similar units this wall is an interior wall separating apartments and therefore does not have openings. Here the same solution for the exterior has been used for the end condition.
Type of construction: Masonry bearing walls; floors: reinforced-concrete slab.
For comparison see the following dwellings: East Boston, Columbia Point, which are similar public housing projects in Boston.

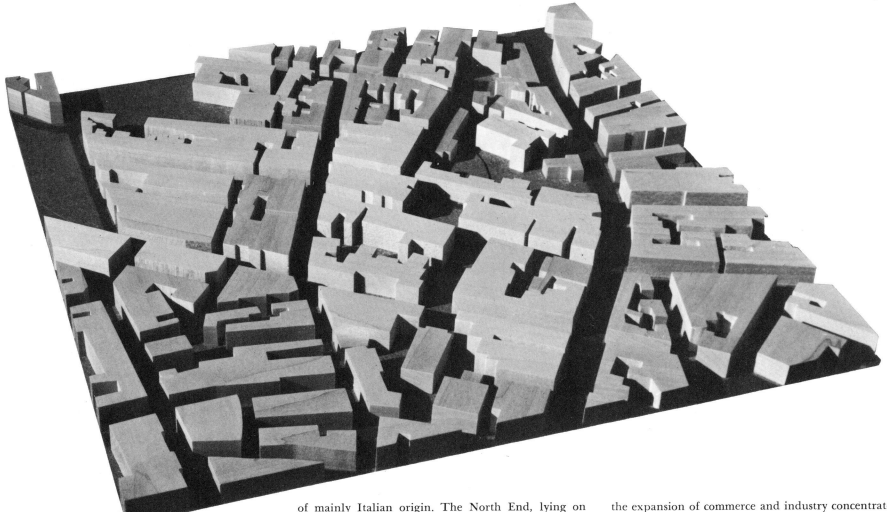

NORTH END, Boston, Massachusetts, U.S.A.

Location: The North End is so called because of its location at the northern tip of the Shawmut peninsula, adjacent to the central business district from which it is now physically separated by the South East elevated expressway. The North End is a densely populated and predominantly low-income area, occupied since 1950 by a relatively stable community of mainly Italian origin. The North End, lying on the slopes of Copp's Hill, is one of the few areas in central Boston built on the original land surface.

Origins: The North End is the oldest part of the City of Boston, and most of the remaining monuments of historic significance are located in this area. The residential area has undergone few basic changes since the 1880's, by which time it had altogether lost its original "court end" character. This was due to the development of the Beacon and Cotton Hill areas at the turn of the nineteenth century in response to the expansion of commerce and industry concentrated along the wharves surrounding the North End. With the great exodus from Ireland during the 1840's the North End became the immigrant center of the city. Toward the end of the century, the then-established Irish started to move out on a significant scale to the two- and three-decker structures built on a large scale in Brighton, Charlestown, East Boston, and Dorchester. The Irish were progressively replaced with Russian Jews and, later, with Italians, many of whom have remained in the now much improved but still densely populated area.

BOSTON INNER HARBOR

NORTH END, Boston
LOCALITY PLAN
Sources: City of Boston, Topographic and Planimetric Survey,
        B.R.A., 1962
Quality of information: Accurate

Layout: The street pattern of the residential area is that of the colonial town, an irregular and approximately rectangular pattern within the semicircular perimeter of the hill. With few exceptions, streets are narrow and there are few open spaces, but intensive use is made of these and of the market streets.

Population: The age-sex pyramid for the North End (in 1960) is almost rectangular; there were the same number of inhabitants between the ages of seventy and seventy-four as there were infants up to the age of four years; and there is relatively little variation among all the five-year steps between. The average age was thirty-two years (60 per cent higher than that for Columbia Point). This suggests a relatively heavy out-migration of young families, and a return of older people (after their families have grown in suburban areas) and of the extended family pattern that develops after a community has been in stable residence for over a generation.

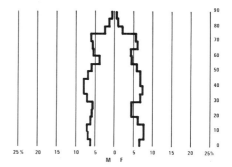

Locality Population Distribution
Census, 1960; tract F-4; population, 3,595
males: M. 1,771; females: F. 1,824
horizontal: percentages; vertical: ages

NORTH END, Boston Air view of the locality: Boston Harbor and piers; John F. Fitzgerald Expressway; Government Center at left center (Urban Renewal project under construction).

BOSTON INNER HARBOR

Land Use: The residential sector is surrounded on three sides by a deteriorated industrial area—like that of East Boston; the location is not suitable for modern industries, few of which depend on immediate harbor facilities. This, however, is in the early stages of conversion into a high-income residential and recreational area. The actual residential area is penetrated by two commercial streets that converge on a street market area adjacent to the expressway.

Incomes: The income distribution (for 1960) is also relatively homogeneous: 53 per cent of households had annual incomes of between U.S.$4,000 and U.S.$8,000 —a lower-middle level at that time. Twelve per cent had relatively high incomes (but none over U.S. $25,000) and 13.5 per cent had very low incomes (under U.S.$2,000 per annum).

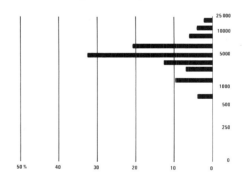

Locality Annual Income Distribution
Census, 1960; tract F-4; households, 973
horizontal: percentages; vertical: dollars

NORTH END, Boston
LOCALITY LAND-USE PATTERN
Sources: Survey, Benninger, 1967
Quality of information: Approximate

AREAS
RESIDENTIAL
COMMERCIAL
INDUSTRIAL

H	Health	Bus (solid line)	Pk	Parking	Ch	Church
PO	Post Office	Rapid Transit	P	Police	R	Recreation
SS	Social Services	(broken line)	F	Fire Department	L	Library
			S	School	U	University

NORTH END, Boston John F. Fitzgerald Expressway; Boston Harbor in the background. Sign reads, "BACK BAY—CALLAHAN TUNNEL (to East Boston and Logan Airport)—CHARLESTOWN—NORTH STATION."

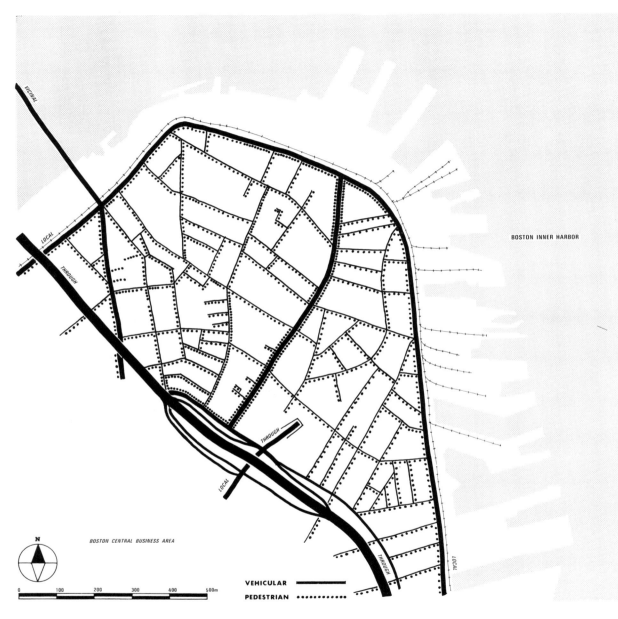

NORTH END, Boston
LOCALITY CIRCULATION PATTERN
Source: Estimate, C. Benninger, 1967
Quality of information: Approximate

Circulation: Public transportation routes are limited to the periphery; most streets are open to vehicular and pedestrian use but, being narrow and mostly one-way, are inconvenient for the former. There are a number of pedestrian passageways, and the area is easier to negotiate on foot.

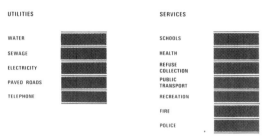

The chart illustrates the approximate availability of utilities and services at four levels: no provision at all, very limited or occasional, generally available but inadequate, and adequate or normal service.

Quality of information: Approximate

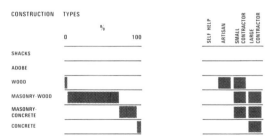

The main dwellings' construction types were grouped as follows: SHACK, ADOBE, WOOD, WOOD AND MASONRY, MASONRY AND CONCRETE, CONCRETE. The main characteristics of these types are described in the introduction.

The building industry was divided into the following groups: SELF-HELP, ARTISAN, SMALL CONTRACTOR, LARGE CONTRACTOR.

The chart shows (1) approximate percentage of each construction type within the total number of dwellings and (2) building group that generally produces each type.

Quality of information: Approximate

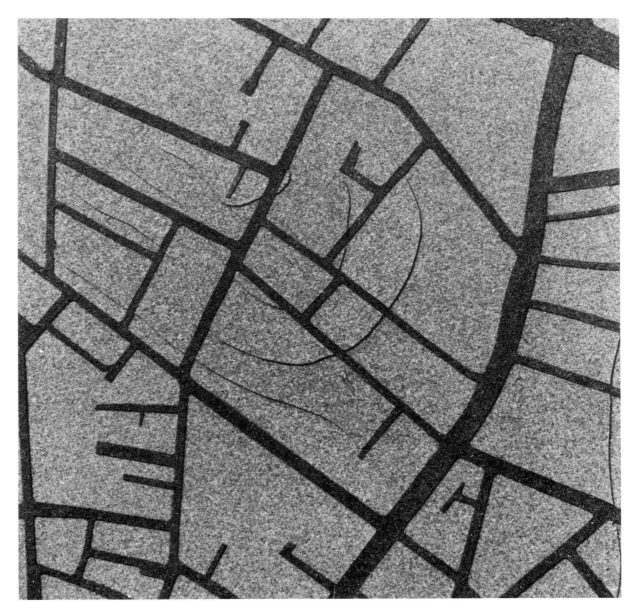

NORTH END, Boston
LOCALITY SEGMENT
400 m × 400 m; scale: 1:2500
Model of raw site showing topography, main circulation layout

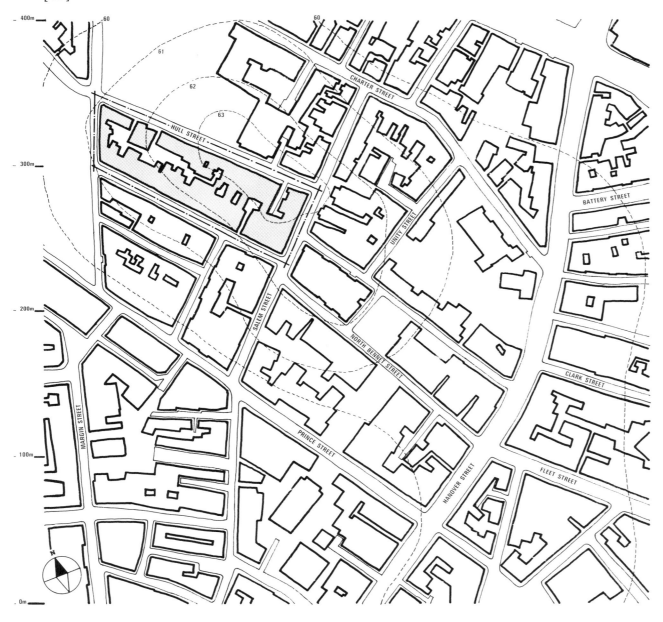

NORTH END, Boston
LOCALITY SEGMENT PLAN
Sources: Sanborn Atlas, Boston 1929 (Periodic Adjustments)
Quality of information: Approximate

Locality Segment: The densely built-up character, as well as the irregular but systematic block layout, is typical of old urban areas. Streets run either parallel with or perpendicular to contours. The blocks are penetrated by many publicly owned alleys and courts, some of which have subdivided the initially small blocks; in consequence, there is a great range of public, semipublic, and private space.

LOCALITY SEGMENT

AREAS

PRIVATE OWNERSHIP	Hectares	Percentage
Dwelling Lots		
Commercial	9.20	57.50
Industrial		
PUBLIC OWNERSHIP		
Community Centers, Parks		
Playgrounds, Schools	1.80	11.24
Streets—Parking	4.70	29.38
Pedestrian Walks	0.30	1.88
Total	16.00	100.00

DENSITIES	Number	Hectares	N/Ha
Lots	555	16.00	34.69
Dwelling Units	1665	16.00	104.06
Families	1665	16.00	104.06
People	6660	16.00	416.25
(4 People/Family)			

Quality of information: Approximate

SELECTED BLOCK

AREAS

PRIVATE OWNERSHIP	Hectares	Percentage
Dwelling Lots		
Commercial	0.53	67.95
Industrial		

PUBLIC OWNERSHIP		
Community Center, Parks	—	—
Playground, Schools	—	—
Streets—Parking	0.25	32.05
Pedestrian Walks		
Total	0.78	100.00

DENSITIES	Number	Hectares	N/Ha
Lots	46	0.78	58.74
Dwelling Units	138	0.78	176.92
Families	138	0.78	176.92
People	552	0.78	707.69
(4 People/Family)			

CIRCULATION RATIO

$$\frac{\text{Circulation Length} = 398 \text{ m}}{\text{Area} \qquad = 0.78 \text{ Ha}} = 510 \text{ m/Ha}$$

Selected block is the area enclosed by the broken line on the Locality Segment plan.

NORTH END, Boston
LOCALITY SEGMENT
400 m × 400 m; scale: 1:2500
Model of developed site showing existing buildings and streets

CHARTER STREET

Dwelling Group: The very dense occupation of the land is evident from the plan and section of the four- and five-story walk-up apartments shown. Clearly, this degree of proximity implies either very close or very distinct and impersonal relationships between neighbors. In addition to the dwellings, a corner store is shown in the plan.

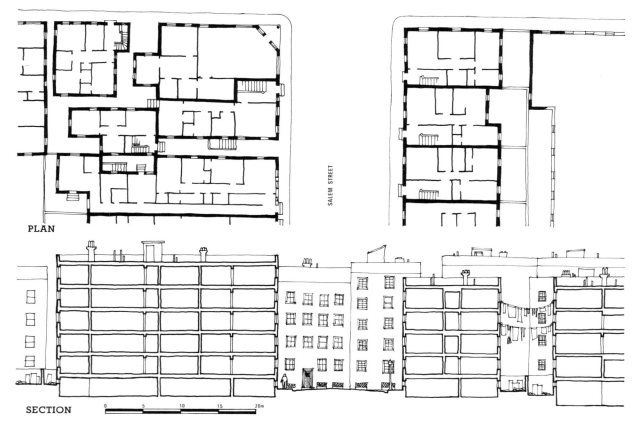

PLAN

SALEM STREET

SECTION

0   5   10   15   20m

NORTH END, Boston
DWELLING GROUP

Sources: Sanborn Atlas, Boston, 1929 (Periodic Additions)
Quality of information: Approximate

NORTH END, Boston Back street. These narrow alleys are about 6 to 8 meters wide. (*opposite page, right*)

Summertime. Men playing table games at Paul Revere Mall on Hanover Street. (*opposite page, top left*)

Atlantic Avenue; fish market; piers; East Boston across the harbor. (*opposite page, bottom left*)

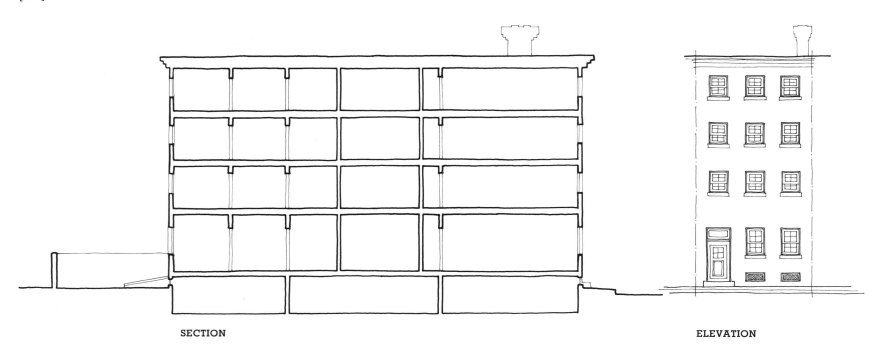

SECTION   ELEVATION

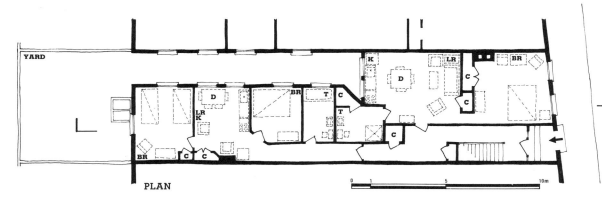

YARD

PLAN

NORTH END, Boston
TYPICAL DWELLING
Sources: Malcolm Davis, Architect, Boston, Sanborn Atlas,
          Boston, 1929 (Periodic Additions)
Quality of information: Approximate

DWELLING-UNIT AREAS

(front unit)	m^2	%
Living (BR, DR, D, LR, K, C)	32.82	70.04
Service (T, L)	4.75	10.14
Circulation	2.92	6.23
Walls	6.37	13.59
Other	—	—
Total Unit Area:	46.86	100.00

Total Lot Area: 6.00 × 28.00 = 168.00 m², semiprivate use

LR	Living Room	K	Kitchen
DR	Dining Room	L	Laundry
D	Dining	T	Toilet—Bathroom
BR	Bedroom	C	Closet

NORTH END, Boston Salem Street: the Italian food market. Merchandise overflows the street when weather permits. North End is Boston's Italian neighborhood.

NORTH END, Boston

Dwelling

Design and development: Private, instant development.

Year of construction: 1910.

Type of dwelling: One-bedroom, walk-up apartment, row house.

Approximate number of people per unit: 2 people.

Approximate dwelling area per person: 24.43 sq. m (front unit).

Layout: A typical developer's flat designed to take maximum advantage of the Building Code by meeting minimum requirements. As a result a narrow side yard "ventilates" and provides "natural light" to "habitable" rooms. There are two apartments per floor in the narrow lot resulting in long corridors that take up a great part of the floor area. This type of plan is very common, not only in Boston, but also in most of the urban areas of the United States. This plan type is frequently used in mirror-image pairs to allow for the maximum open side yard space between buildings for light and ventilation.

Facilities: Kitchen, dining, living areas are combined in one room; bathroom, domestic hot and cold water, basement laundry, heating, electricity, telephone, closets are provided.

Components: Double hung windows.

Type of construction: Masonry bearing walls of brick, lath, and plaster interior partitions; wood floors and roof.

For comparison see the following dwellings: South End, which is another common type of row house.

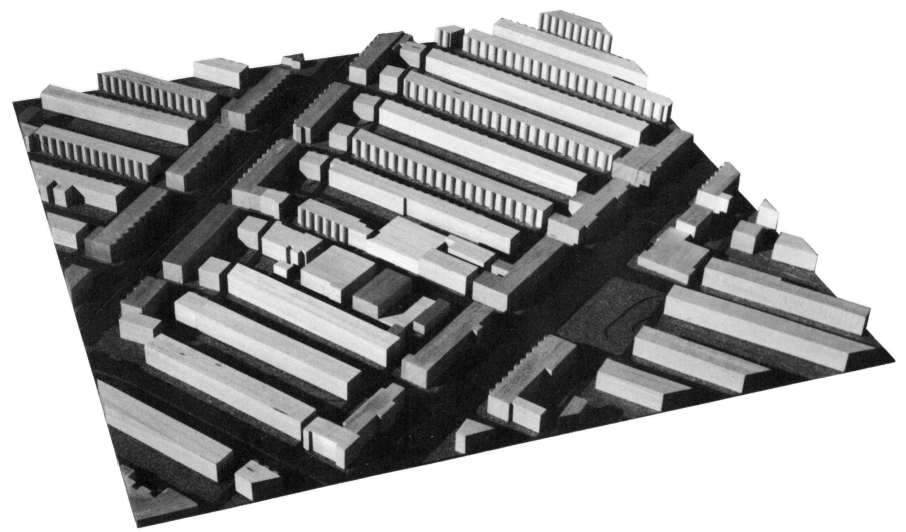

SOUTH END, Boston, Massachusetts, U.S.A.

Location: The area of the city of Boston known as the South End is adjacent to the central business district.

Origins: Originally Boston was attached to Roxbury only by a very narrow neck of land along which ran Washington Street. During the early nineteenth century this was gradually widened by the filling of Back Bay. The South End was built up in the 1850's and 1860's, mostly with row houses but also with a full complement of churches, schools, hotels, and hospitals. Before the filling of the South Bay the shore line and bay was a fashionable recreation area, and the locality was dominated by single-family houses. After the bay was filled for industrial use, the occupancy of the locality changed. The single-family dwellings were converted into apartments and rooming houses for low-income people. At the present time, because of the lack of available housing to meet the demand and the proximity of the locality to the central business district, high-income families are forcing the poor to move elsewhere.

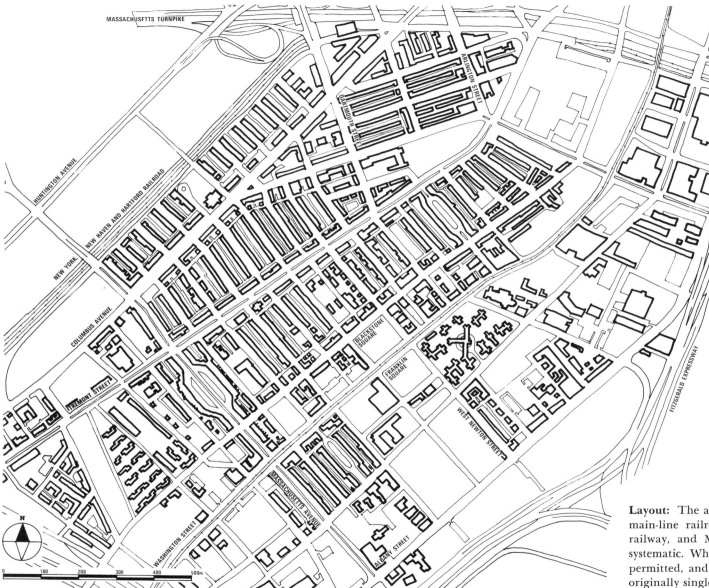

SOUTH END, Boston
LOCALITY PLAN
Sources: City of Boston, Topographic and Planimetric Survey,
          B.R.A., 1962
Quality of information: Accurate

Layout: The area within the rectangle formed by the main-line railroad and turnpike, the local elevated railway, and Massachusetts Avenue is uniform and systematic. Where main streets and boundaries have permitted, and in the majority of cases, the blocks of originally single-family row houses are long with their short sides facing the main traffic streets. The system ensures a maximum flow along the latter and, therefore, past the sites for commercial activities. The blocks are subdivided by access alleys giving access to the backs of all plots.

SOUTH END, Boston Air view of street and block pattern of row housing. Compare with plan of segment of locality. (1968)

Land Use: A concentration of light industry and a hospital complex border the south side of the locality, but there are also scattered industrial buildings in other sections; commerce is concentrated along the four main through streets. There are a large number of community facilities in the area—the survey shows 26 churches and 12 schools.

AREAS

RESIDENTIAL

COMMERCIAL

INDUSTRIAL

SOUTH END, Boston
LOCALITY LAND-USE PATTERN
Sources: South End Renewal Plan, B.R.A.
Quality of information: Accurate

H Health	Bus **(solid line)**	**Pk** Parking	**Ch** Church
PO Post Office	Rapid Transit	**P** Police	**R** Recreation
SS Social Services	**(broken line)**	**F** Fire Department	**L** Library
		S School	**U** University

SOUTH END, Boston Elevated public transit line over Washington Street. Metered parallel parking on both sides of the street leaves two marrow lanes for the traffic. *(right)* 1956

Union Park with Prudential's Office and hotel buildings in the background. Prudential Building with 52 floors is the tallest structure in Boston. (1965) *(top)*

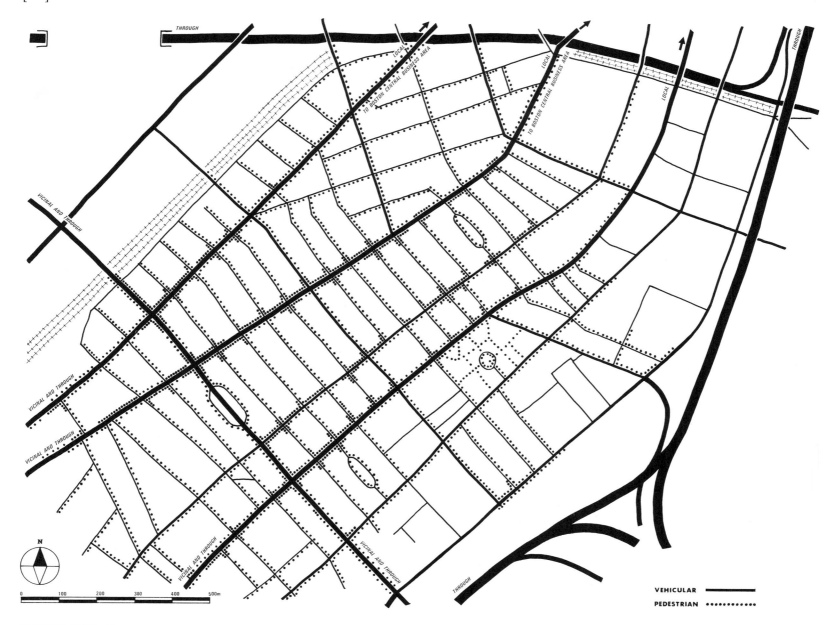

SOUTH END, Boston
LOCALITY CIRCULATION PATTERN
Source: Estimate, B. Cavin, 1967
Quality of information: Tentative

Circulation: Major, limited-access highways bound three sides of the locality separating the locality from the city's central business district. The fourth side is bounded by a main local and vicinal circulator that serves as a meshing line with the adjacent community. The important locality circulation is along parallel streets that run the length of the locality. The secondary circulation is along the cross streets.

The chart illustrates the approximate availability of utilities and services at four levels: no provision at all, very limited or occasional, generally available but inadequate, and adequate or normal service.

Quality of information: Approximate

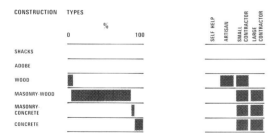

The main dwellings' construction types were grouped as follows: SHACK, ADOBE, WOOD, WOOD AND MASONRY, MASONRY AND CONCRETE, CONCRETE. The main characteristics of these types are described in the introduction.

The building industry was divided into the following groups: SELF-HELP, ARTISAN, SMALL CONTRACTOR, LARGE CONTRACTOR.

The chart shows (1) approximate percentage of each construction type within the total number of dwellings and (2) building group that generally produces each type.

Quality of information: Approximate

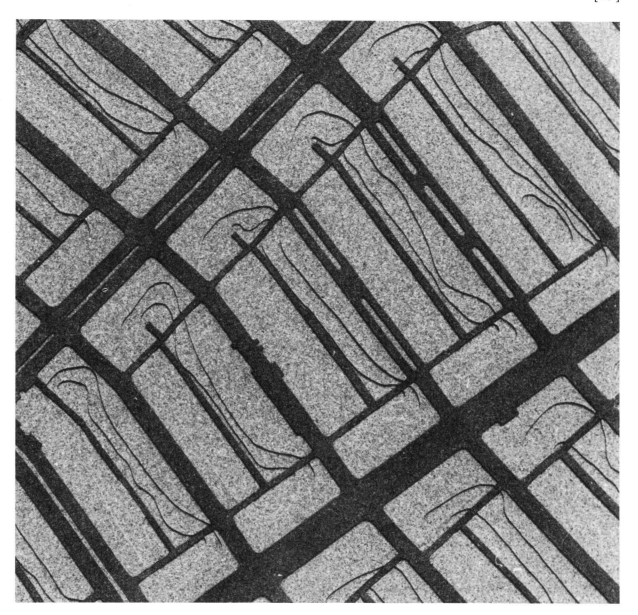

SOUTH END, Boston
LOCALITY SEGMENT
400 m × 400 m; scale: 1:2500
Model of raw site showing topography, main circulation layout

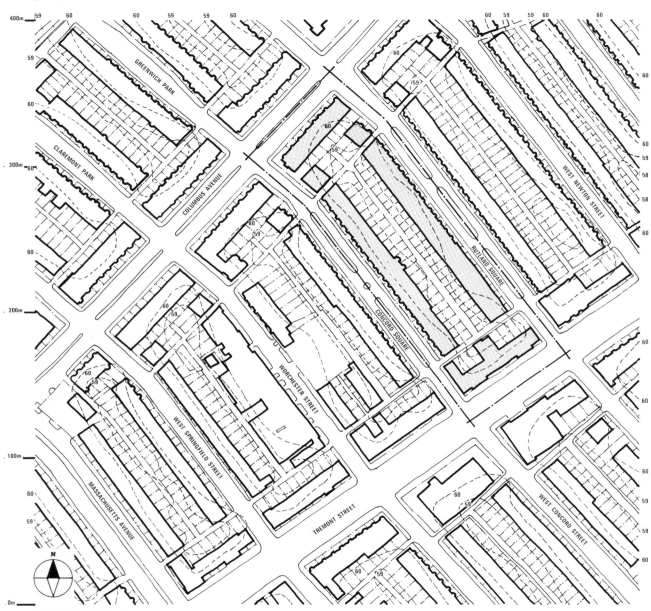

Locality Segment: The land subdivision is typical of row-house development. The rectangular blocks are divided into narrow lots served by local streets at the front. In addition, service alleys penetrate the center of the block, providing access to the rear of each lot. It is evident that the development is on filled land because the streets are higher than the interior of the blocks.

LOCALITY SEGMENT

AREAS

PRIVATE OWNERSHIP	Hectares	Percentage
Dwelling Lots	8.3	51.88
Commercial	1.5	9.37
Industrial	0.4	2.50

PUBLIC OWNERSHIP		
Community Centers, Parks Playgrounds, Schools	0.4	2.50
Streets—Parking Pedestrian Walks	5.4	33.75
Total	16.00	100.00

DENSITIES	Number	Hectares	N/Ha
Lots	502	16	31.38
Dwelling Units	1600	16	100.00
Families	1250	16	78.13
People	2700	16	168.75
(2 People/Family)			

Quality of information: Approximate

SOUTH END, Boston
LOCALITY SEGMENT PLAN
Sources: City of Boston, Topographic and Planimetric Survey,
    B.R.A., 1962
Quality of information: Approximate

SELECTED BLOCK

AREAS

PRIVATE OWNERSHIP	Hectares	Percentage
Dwelling Lots	1.15	59.90
Commercial	—	—
Industrial	—	—

PUBLIC OWNERSHIP		
Community Center, Parks	—	—
Playground, Schools	—	—
Streets—Parking		
Pedestrian Walks	0.77	40.10
Total	1.92	100.00

DENSITIES	Number	Hectares	N/Ha
Lots	69	1.92	35.94
Dwelling Units	276	1.92	143.75
Families	230	1.92	119.79
People	460	1.92	239.58
(2 People/Family)			

CIRCULATION RATIO

$$\frac{\text{Circulation Length} = 650 \text{ m}}{\text{Area} \qquad = 1.92 \text{ Ha}} = 338 \text{ m/Ha}$$

Selected block is the area enclosed by the broken line on the Locality Segment plan.

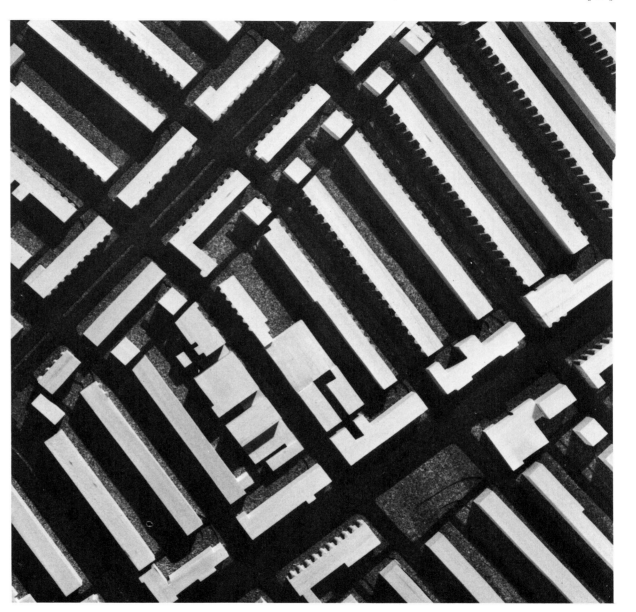

SOUTH END, Boston
LOCALITY SEGMENT
400 m × 400 m; scale: 1:2500
Model of developed site showing existing buildings and streets

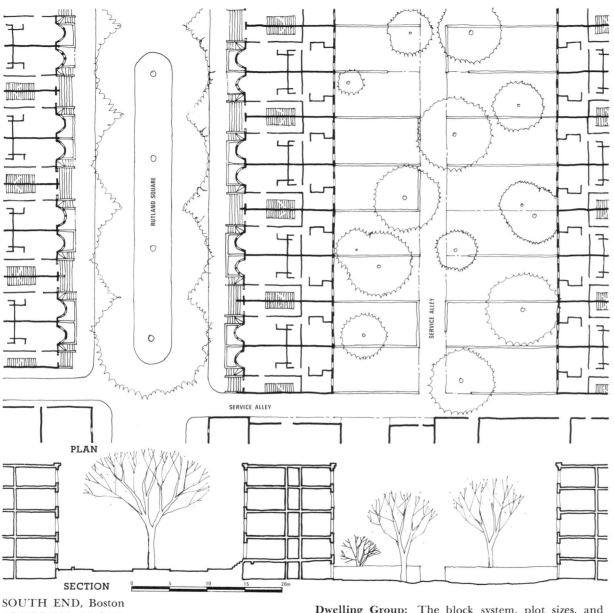

RUTLAND SQUARE

SERVICE ALLEY

SERVICE ALLEY

PLAN

SECTION

0   5   10   15   20m

SOUTH END, Boston
DWELLING GROUP

Sources: City of Boston, Topographic and Planimetric Survey,
    B.R.A., 1962
Quality of information: Approximate

Dwelling Group: The block system, plot sizes, and
dwelling types are fully standardized, but the street
lengths vary appreciably, and the residential streets
are not straight from one block to the next; the now

very large trees in the "squares" and the gardens also
provide variety. The alley system provided for the
segregation of service activities and formal family and
social living. The plots in the segment shown are
relatively small: 26 m deep × 6 m wide (156 sq m).

Population: Sixty per cent of the 3,262 persons registered in the 1960 census were males with an average
age of forty-five years; the 40 per cent female population had an average age of forty-seven years (the
largest of the five-year age groups was that of sixty-five
to fifty-nine).

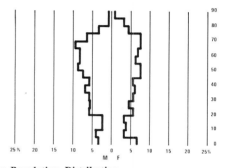

Locality Population Distribution
Census, 1960; tract L-1; population, 3,262
males: M. 1,932; females: F. 1,330
horizontal: percentages; vertical: ages

Incomes: The average household income in 1960 was
U.S. $2,284—30 per cent of the average for the Bos-
ton metropolitan area. No households with incomes
of over $8,000 were registered.

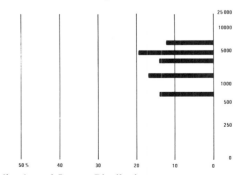

Locality Annual Income Distribution
Census, 1960; tract L-1; households, 552
horizontal: percentages; vertical: dollars

SOUTH END, Boston Row houses, brick bearing walls, wood framing. Lots are about 6 meters wide. (*left*)

City park—Franklin Square. Elevated public transit line in the background. (*top right*)

Residential street; row houses; central strip for trees. Street is used for parallel parking. (*bottom right*)

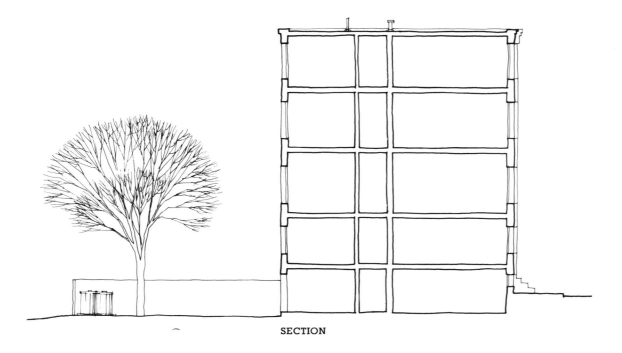

SECTION

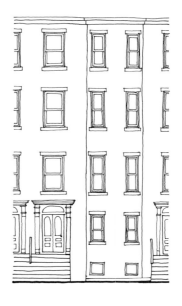

ELEVATION

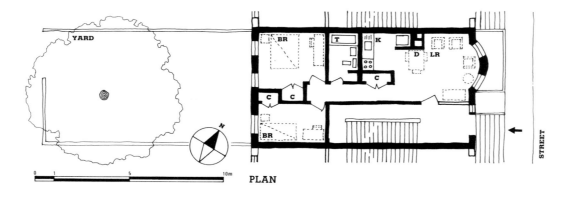

PLAN

SOUTH END, Boston
TYPICAL DWELLING
Sources: Inferred from plan, Harris Associates, 1965
Quality of information: Approximate

DWELLING-UNIT AREAS

	m^2	%
Living (BR, DR, D, LR, K, C)	34.78	61.09
Service (T, L)	5.66	9.78
Circulation	3.68	6.37
Walls	13.78	22.76
Other	—	—
Total Unit Area:	57.90	100.00

Total Lot Area: $6.00 \times 24.00 = 144.00$ m², semiprivate use

LR	Living Room	**K**	Kitchen
DR	Dining Room	**L**	Laundry
D	Dining	**T**	Toilet—Bathroom
BR	Bedroom	**C**	Closet

SOUTH END, Boston Row housing along Rutland Square. Masonry bearing walls, wood framing. Bay windows are characteristic of row houses in Boston. (*right*)

Service alley behind row houses: wood fences, dilapidated gardens. (*top*)

SOUTH END, Boston

Dwelling

Design and development: Private, instant development.

Year of construction: circa 1860.

Type of dwelling: Originally a single-family row house; now two-bedroom walk-up apartments.

Approximate number of people per unit: 3 people.

Approximate dwelling area per person: 19.30 sq. m.

Layout: Originally designed and built as medium-high income single-family houses, the great majority were either subdivided into separate apartments or used as rooming houses, a trend that is beginning to reverse itself in the 1960's. The present building has one apartment per floor served by one stairway; a compact well-designed plan in a 6 m wide lot; a small corridor provides privacy for the bedrooms and bath. This type of plan is also very common not only in Boston but in most urban areas of the United States as well.

Facilities: Back-to-back kitchen-bathroom plumbing; both are interior rooms with forced ventilation; the small kitchen opens into the dining-living area; domestic hot and cold water, central heating; electricity, telephone are provided.

Components: Double hung windows looking into the front and back yard; bay windows in the front and sometimes in the back are a common feature.

Type of construction: Masonry bearing walls of brick; interior partitions of lath and plaster on wood studs; wood floors and roof.

For comparison see the following dwellings: North End, which is another common type of row house but developed for a lower income market.

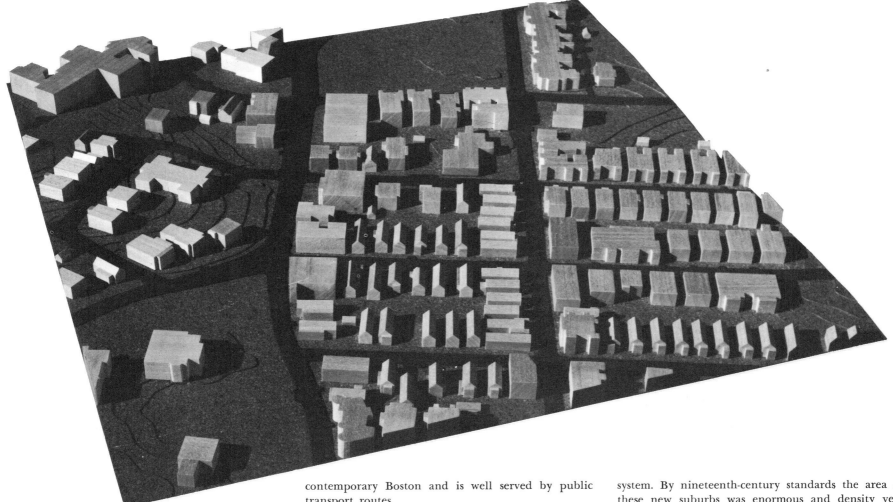

WASHINGTON PARK, Boston, Massachusetts, U.S.A.

Location: Washington Park is a section of Roxbury, a district with a predominantly black population, 4 kilometers southwest from the central business district. The locality is well within the built-up area of

contemporary Boston and is well served by public transport routes.

Origins: Before the industrial expansion of Boston of the mid-nineteenth century, Roxbury was an independent town; in the latter part of the century Roxbury became a fashionable residential district beyond the radius of the old pedestrian city. The development of the "streetcar suburbs" of Roxbury, West Roxbury, and Dorchester after 1855 is analogous to the contemporary development of areas such as Lincoln and Concord, opened up by the freeway

system. By nineteenth-century standards the area of these new suburbs was enormous and density very low (60,000 in an area of over 25 square miles in 1870, increasing to 227,000 in 1900). Lower-middle-class housing construction began in Roxbury in 1887, and the area continued to gain population during the first decade of the twentieth century. The change began between the world wars, during which Roxbury lost population, substantially; this was replaced by the even greater gains after 1940, with the influx of a low-income, predominantly Afro-American minority.

WASHINGTON PARK, Boston
LOCALITY PLAN
Sources: City of Boston, Topographic and Planimetric Survey,
      B.R.A., 1962
Quality of information: Accurate

Layout: Washington Park is a typical nineteenth-century suburban subdivision for middle- and upper-income families, with the basic rectangular grid greatly modified by the topography. Several of the largest properties take advantage of the hills and views, creating a series of dead-end streets and loops more typical of twentieth-century subdivision patterns.

Population: The asymmetrics of the age-sex pyramid, showing a substantially higher proportion of young adult females, could be explained by the existence of a large proportion of fatherless families and the frequently reported reluctance of young Afro-Americans to be registered in the census. The pyramid shows a higher-than-average proportion of young families.

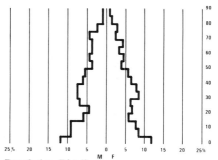

Locality Population Distribution
Census, 1960; tract V-6A; population, 4,925
males: M. 2,289; females: F. 2,636
horizontal: percentages; vertical: ages

WASHINGTON PARK, Boston Air View. Detached dwellings in narrow lots about 9 meters wide. The trees are taller than the 3- to 4-story dwellings. (1968) *(opposite page)*

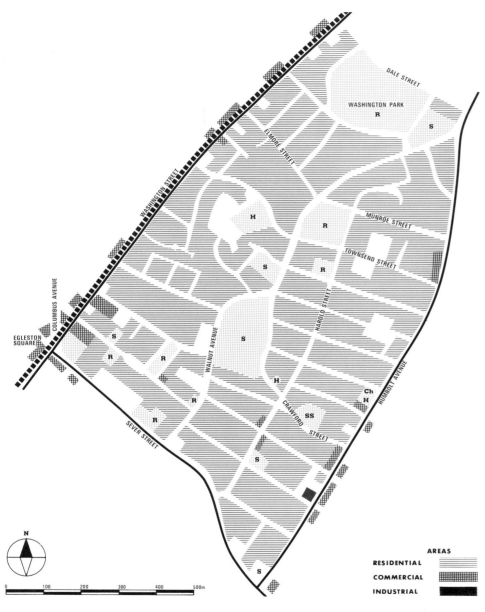

Land Use: The area is largely residential; there is no industry or significant commercial activity, except along the main traffic arteries. The area is relatively well provided with open space, located between the bordering arteries.

Incomes: (1960) The average is low, approximately U.S.$4,500 per household, per annum, 30 per cent below the metropolitan average. Twenty-one per cent would be excluded from public housing by their incapacity to pay the average rent for a two-bedroom apartment. Less than 10 per cent were in the middle-income category in 1960.

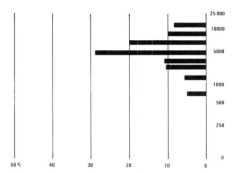

Locality Annual Income Distribution
Census, 1960; tract V-6A; households, 1148
horizontal: percentages; vertical: dollars

WASHINGTON PARK, Boston
LOCALITY LAND-USE PATTERN
Sources: Survey, Henry, 1967
Quality of information: Approximate

H Health	Bus (solid line)	
PO Post Office	Rapid Transit	
SS Social Services	(broken line)	

Pk Parking   Ch Church
P Police   R Recreation
F Fire Department   L Library
S School   U University

AREAS
RESIDENTIAL
COMMERCIAL
INDUSTRIAL

WASHINGTON PARK, Boston Corner on Washington Street; elevated rapid-transit station in Egleston Square. Cars parked in front of sign, "NO PARKING ANY TIME." (1968)

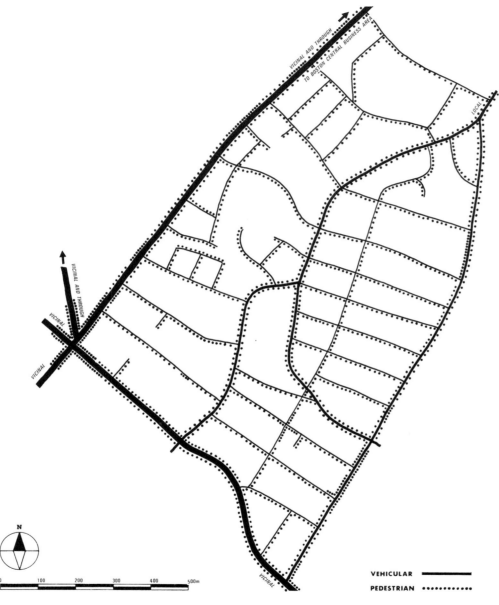

WASHINGTON PARK, Boston
LOCALITY CIRCULATION PATTERN
Source: Estimate, G. Henry, 1967
Quality of information: Tentative

VEHICULAR ▬▬▬▬
PEDESTRIAN ••••••••••

Circulation: All public access routes are open to both vehicular and pedestrian traffic. The locality is bounded on two sides by through traffic routes; the other more heavily used streets are those oriented to the city center.

The chart illustrates the approximate availability of utilities and services at four levels: no provision at all, very limited or occasional, generally available but inadequate, and adequate or normal service.

Quality of information: Approximate

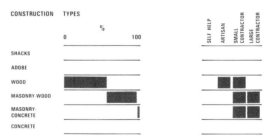

The main dwellings' construction types were grouped as follows: SHACK, ADOBE, WOOD, WOOD AND MASONRY, MASONRY AND CONCRETE, CONCRETE. The main characteristics of these types are described in the introduction.

The building industry was divided into the following groups: SELF-HELP, ARTISAN, SMALL CONTRACTOR, LARGE CONTRACTOR.

The chart shows (1) approximate percentage of each construction type within the total number of dwellings and (2) building group that generally produces each type.

Quality of information: Approximate

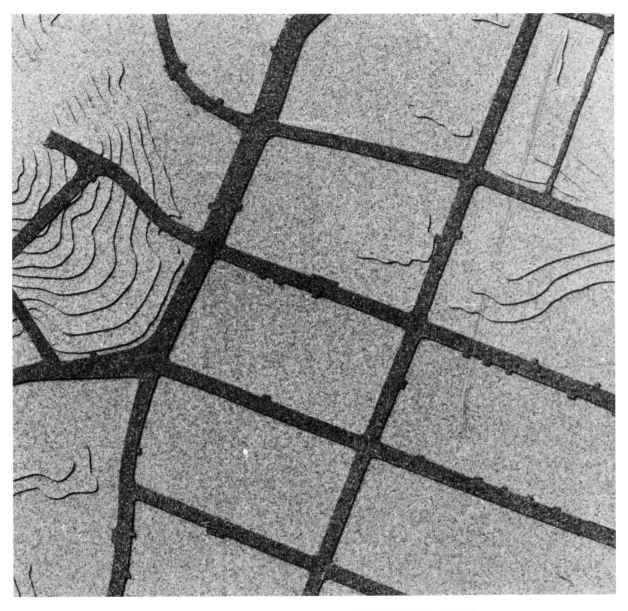

WASHINGTON PARK, Boston
LOCALITY SEGMENT
400 m × 400 m; scale: 1:2500
Model of raw site showing topography, main circulation layout

Locality Segment: Individual properties, as well as the blocks, vary considerably in size and shape. There are a few access alleys of the type common in layouts of the earlier part of the nineteenth century (see South End and Charlestown).

LOCALITY SEGMENT

AREAS

PRIVATE OWNERSHIP	Hectares	Percentage
Dwelling Lots	8.17	51.06
Commercial	—	—
Industrial	—	—
PUBLIC OWNERSHIP		
Community Centers, Parks Playgrounds, Schools	4.26	26.63
Streets—Parking Pedestrian Walks	3.57	22.31
Total	16.00	100.00

DENSITIES	Number	Hectares	N/Ha
Lots	169	16.00	10.56
Dwelling Units	495	16.00	30.94
Families	495	16.00	30.94
People	1980	16.00	123.75
(4 People/Family)			

Quality of information: Approximate

WASHINGTON PARK, Boston
LOCALITY SEGMENT PLAN
Sources: City of Boston, Topographic and Planimetric Survey,
    B.R.A., 1962
Quality of information: Accurate

SELECTED BLOCK

AREAS

PRIVATE OWNERSHIP	Hectares	Percentage
Dwelling Lots	0.87	73.11
Commercial	—	—
Industrial	—	—

PUBLIC OWNERSHIP		
Community Center, Parks	—	—
Playground, Schools	—	—
Streets—Parking Pedestrian Walks	0.32	26.89
Total	1.19	100.00

DENSITIES	Number	Hectares	N/Ha
Lots	18	1.19	15.13
Dwelling Units	69	1.19	57.98
Families	69	1.19	57.98
People	276	1.19	231.93
(4 People/Family)			

CIRCULATION RATIO

$$\frac{\text{Circulation Length} = 220 \text{ m}}{\text{Area} \qquad = 1.19 \text{ Ha}} = 185 \text{ m/Ha}$$

Selected block is the area enclosed by the broken line on the Locality Segment plan.

WASHINGTON PARK, Boston
LOCALITY SEGMENT
400 m × 400 m; scale: 1:2500
Model of developed site showing existing buildings and streets

Dwelling Group: The dwellings are set back from the streets with, generally, little land on either side. The rear yards, however, are large. Off-street parking is provided in many cases.

HAROLD STREET

HOLWORTHY STREET

PLAN

SECTION

WASHINGTON PARK, Boston
DWELLING GROUP
Sources: Inferred from Architectural Plans, B.R.A., 1965
Quality of information: Approximate

WASHINGTON PARK, Boston Residential street. Big trees dominate the scene. (1968)

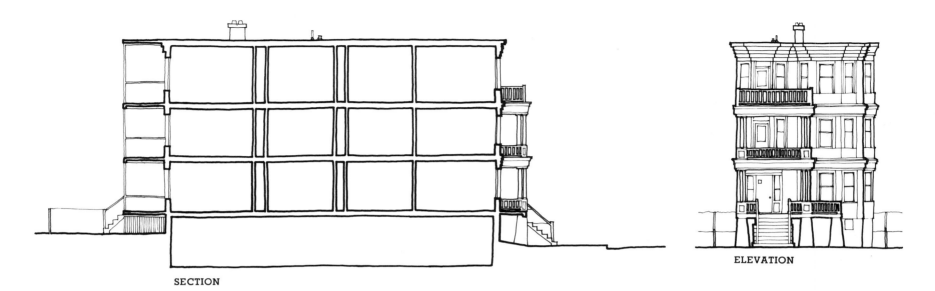

SECTION

ELEVATION

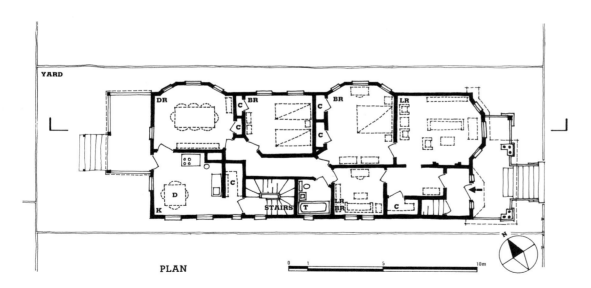

PLAN

0   1   5   10m

WASHINGTON PARK, Boston
TYPICAL DWELLING
Sources: Plans, B.R.A., 1965
Quality of information: Approximate

DWELLING-UNIT AREAS

	m^2	%
Living (BR, DR, D, LR, K, C)	69.63	58.57
Service (T, L)	7.18	6.04
Circulation	11.00	9.25
Walls	25.07	21.09
Other (porch)	6.00	5.05
Total Unit Area:	118.88	100.00

Total Lot Area: $9.00 \times 27.00 = 243.00$ m², semiprivate use

LR	Living Room	**K**	Kitchen
DR	Dining Room	**L**	Laundry
D	Dining	**T**	Toilet—Bathroom
BR	Bedroom	**C**	Closet

WASHINGTON PARK, Boston Condemned wood single-family dwelling. Detached dwellings occupy almost the whole lot leaving narrow spaces between buildings, which sometimes are used as parking driveways.

WASHINGTON PARK, Boston

Dwelling

Design and development: Private, instant development.

Year of construction: 1910.

Type of dwelling: Two-bedroom, walk-up apartment, detached house.

Approximate number of people per unit: 4 people.

Approximate dwelling area per person: 29.72 sq. m.

Layout: A typical three-story building with an apartment on each floor; the building is long and narrow to fit tightly in the lot, leaving very little space around it; there is a short corridor; however, some rooms are used for circulation. There are no interior rooms. Front and back porches exist on all floors. The back porches are commonly used to hang laundry.

Facilities: A generous kitchen space with dining table, but very limited counter work space; bathroom; laundry in basement, domestic hot and cold water; central heating; electricity, telephone; generous closets.

Components: Double hung windows, bay windows in three rooms.

Type of construction: Wooden structure, balloon-frame type; the basement has masonry walls and accommodates the boiler as well as other bulky heating equipment, but at the same time it is space gained for little cost. In effect, since the foundations need to go (1.20 m) below the frost line, by excavating under the house and raising the first floor another 1.20 m one entire floor is gained.

For comparison see the following dwellings: Cambridgeport, which is a similar type of dwelling.

COLUMBIA POINT, Boston, Massachusetts, U.S.A.

Location: Columbia Point, like many parts of Boston, was mainly tideland originally; and, in 1967–1968, this largely artificial peninsula jutting into Boston Harbor had an area of about 160 hectares.

The dominant features on this largely desolate land is the public housing project of the same name. The other principal occupant is Boston College High School (which has no connection with the project population). The area is a little over 3 kilometers from the central business district and is connected to it by subway and expressways, one kilometer distant from the farthest block in the project.

Origins: The Columbia Point Housing Project was built in 1954 by the Boston Housing Authority. In 1967–1968, there were no neighborhood schools or commercial facilities in the locality; when first constructed, there were no shopping facilities in the vicinity so that residents had to be provided with a free weekend bus service to South Boston. Studies have been made by the Boston Redevelopment Authority for the extension of the area and its development for private middle-income housing, a large high school, and community and recreational facilities.

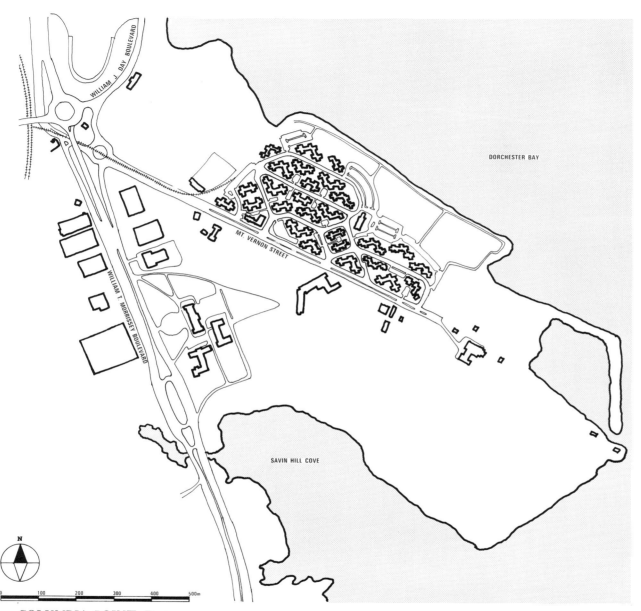

COLUMBIA POINT, Boston
LOCALITY PLAN
Sources: City of Boston, Topographic and Planimetric Survey,
        B.R.A., 1962
Quality of information: Accurate

Layout: The Project area is a dense conglomeration of apartment buildings, mostly seven stories high. The layout was probably determined by efforts to achieve economy through high density and inexpensive forms of construction. The project is a planned instant development having a "picturesque" layout which fails to avoid monotony.

Population: The total population in 1967, was 5,837 in 1,433 households (just over 4 persons per household). The 1959 census tract for the locality, which includes a relatively large proportion of higher-income residents of an adjacent area, may not reflect the characteristics of the Project population very accurately. The youthfulness of the population (average age nineteen) and the 10 per cent bias of the population between the ages of twenty and forty-four toward the female side are both likely to be the products of the special characteristics of the Project population. There is a high proportion of incomplete families in this predominantly Afro-American neighborhood, and the ratio of children to adults is appreciably higher than the metropolitan norm.

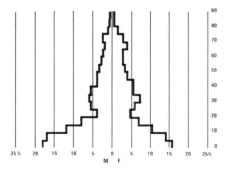

Locality Population Distribution
Census, 1960; tract T-1; population, 9,770
males: M. 4,563; females: F. 5,207
horizontal: percentages; vertical: ages

COLUMBIA POINT, Boston Air view. Public housing in the center; Dorchester Bay at the top; school building and playground at the bottom.

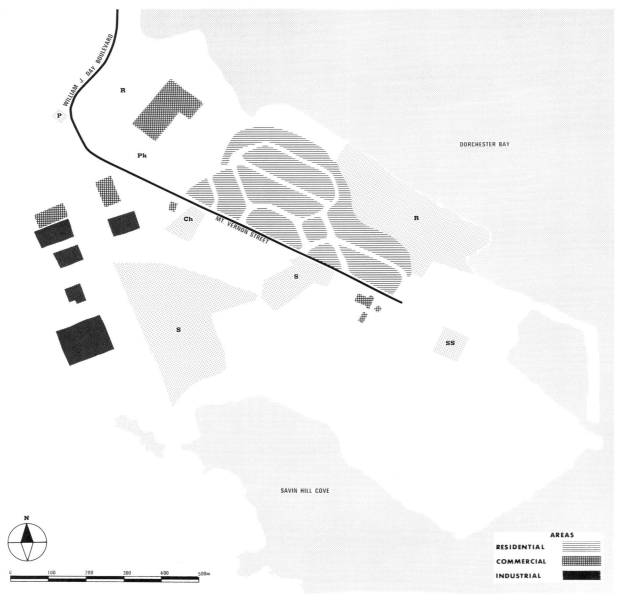

Land Use: About 20 per cent of the 11 hectares of the Project area is used for the apartment buildings and their limited landscaping, drying yards, and parking areas. Nineteen per cent of the remaining area is devoted to streets (about 10 meters wide) and sidewalks (about 1.75 meters wide) and 36 per cent is left for park and recreation space. There are no schools or commercial facilities within the Project itself, and there is no large area or building designated as a community center.

Incomes: The same qualification of the data for population applies to that for incomes. The high proportion of household incomes below U.S.$3,000 per annum (33.3 per cent) as against 19.5 and 18 per cent in the North End and East Boston respectively, is also due undoubtedly to the bias of the Project population. In 1968, 70 per cent of the households were receiving welfare payments.

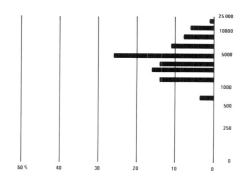

Locality Annual Income Distribution
Census, 1960; tract T-1; households, 2,127
horizontal: percentages; vertical: dollars

COLUMBIA POINT, Boston
LOCALITY LAND-USE PATTERN
Sources: Columbia Point, Feasibility Study, FS-89, B.R.A., 1964
Quality of information: Accurate

H	Health	Bus **(solid line)**	**Pk**	Parking	**Ch** Church
PO	Post Office	Rapid Transit	**P**	Police	**R** Recreation
SS	Social Services	**(broken line)**	**F**	Fire Department	**L** Library
			S	School	**U** University

AREAS
RESIDENTIAL
COMMERCIAL
INDUSTRIAL

COLUMBIA POINT, Boston Parking facing the Dorchester
Bay; high-rise apartments (7 stories) in the background. (1968)

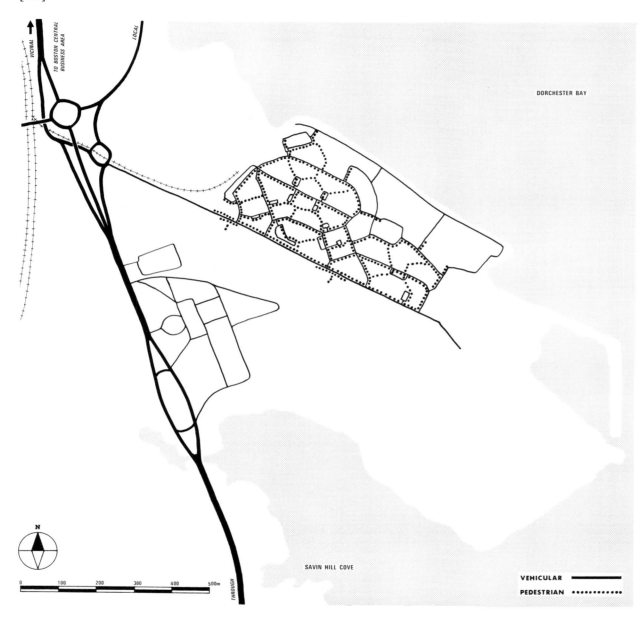

DORCHESTER BAY

SAVIN HILL COVE

VEHICULAR ━━━━
PEDESTRIAN •••••••••••

COLUMBIA POINT, Boston
LOCALITY CIRCULATION PATTERN
Source: Estimate, F. Smith, 1967
Quality of information: Approximate

Circulation: There is free pedestrian circulation around and between the individual apartment blocks, but vehicular circulation is limited to the rather irregular street pattern breaking the area up into islands or blocks of different sizes—the smallest a triangle enclosing one apartment building, the largest enclosing five. All traffic, pedestrian and vehicular, must use the long, straight street (over one kilometer) bordering the longer side of the Project area and connecting it with the freeways, the subway, and the new (1967) shopping center. Many residents use private automobiles for transportation to work.

The chart illustrates the approximate availability of utilities and services at four levels: no provision at all, very limited or occasional, generally available but inadequate, and adequate or normal service.

Quality of information: Approximate

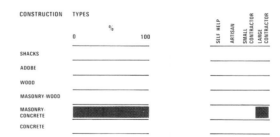

The main dwellings' construction types were grouped as follows: SHACK, ADOBE, WOOD, WOOD AND MASONRY, MASONRY AND CONCRETE, CONCRETE. The main characteristics of these types are described in the introduction.

The building industry was divided into the following groups: SELF-HELP, ARTISAN, SMALL CONTRACTOR, LARGE CONTRACTOR.

The chart shows (1) approximate percentage of each construction type within the total number of dwellings and (2) building group that generally produces each type.

Quality of information: Approximate

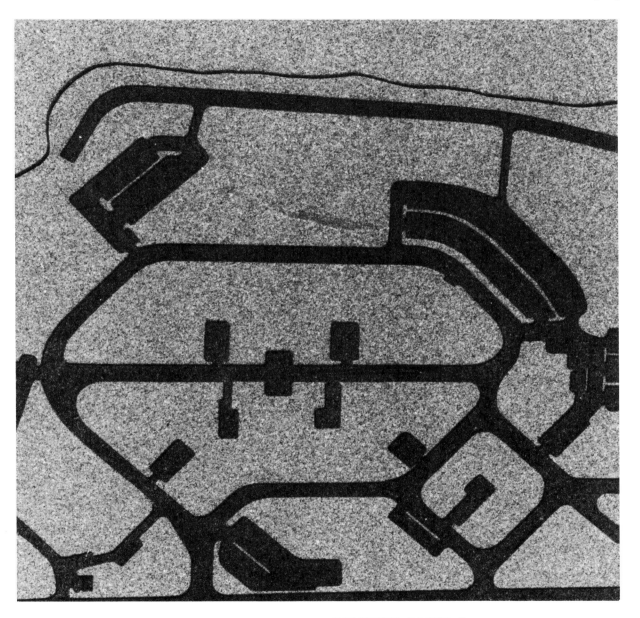

COLUMBIA POINT, Boston
LOCALITY SEGMENT
400 m × 400 m; scale: 1:2500
Model of raw site showing topography, main circulation layout

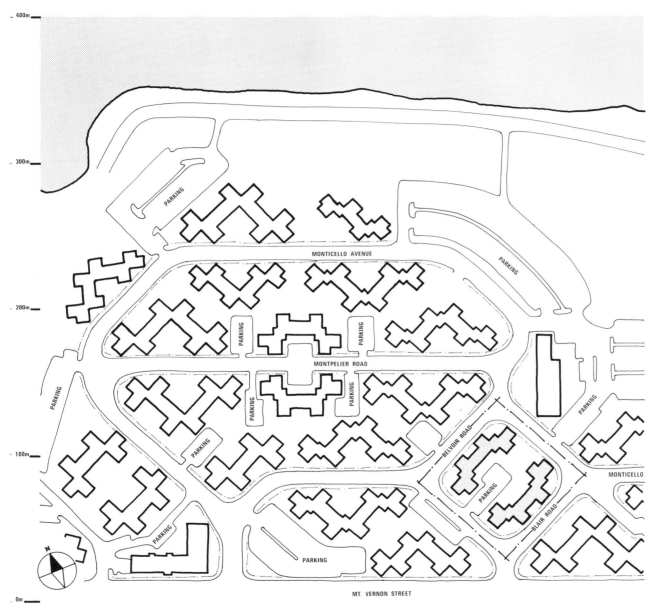

Locality Segment: The confusing uniformity and arbitrariness of the layout is striking at this scale; the contrast between the mazelike and very constricted spaces between the buildings and the extensive and indefinite open space around the mass of blocks is also emphasized.

LOCALITY SEGMENT

AREAS

PRIVATE OWNERSHIP	Hectares	Percentage
Dwelling Lots	—	—
Commercial	—	—
Industrial	—	—

PUBLIC OWNERSHIP		
Public Housing (Buildings)	2.12	13.25
Community Centers, Parks Playgrounds, Schools	6.73	42.06
Streets—Parking Pedestrian Walks	4.75	29.69
Water	2.40	15.00
Total	16.00	100.00

DENSITIES	Number	Hectares	N/Ha
Lots			
Dwelling Units	1200	16.00	75.00
Families	1200	16.00	75.00
People	4800	16.00	300.00
(4 People/Family)			

Quality of information: Approximate

COLUMBIA POINT, Boston
LOCALITY SEGMENT PLAN
Sources: City of Boston, Topographic and Planimetric Survey,
   B.R.A., 1962; Description of public housing, Castle
   Square Relocation Program, B.R.A.   Quality of information: Accurate

SELECTED BLOCK

AREAS

PRIVATE OWNERSHIP	*Hectares*	*Percentage*
Dwelling Lots	—	—
Commercial	—	—
Industrial	—	—

PUBLIC OWNERSHIP		
Public Housing (Buildings)	0.13	19.70
Community Center, Parks Playground, Schools	0.26	39.40
Streets—Parking	0.27	40.90
Pedestrian Walks	—	—
Total	0.66	100.00

DENSITIES	*Number*	*Hectares*	*N/Ha*
Lots	1	0.6	1.67
Dwelling Units	112	0.6	186.67
Families	112	0.6	186.67
People (4 People/Family)	448	0.6	746.67

CIRCULATION RATIO

$$\frac{\text{Circulation Length} = 198 \text{ m}}{\text{Area} \qquad = 0.66 \text{ Ha}} = 300 \text{ m/Ha}$$

Selected block is the area enclosed by the broken line on the Locality Segment plan.

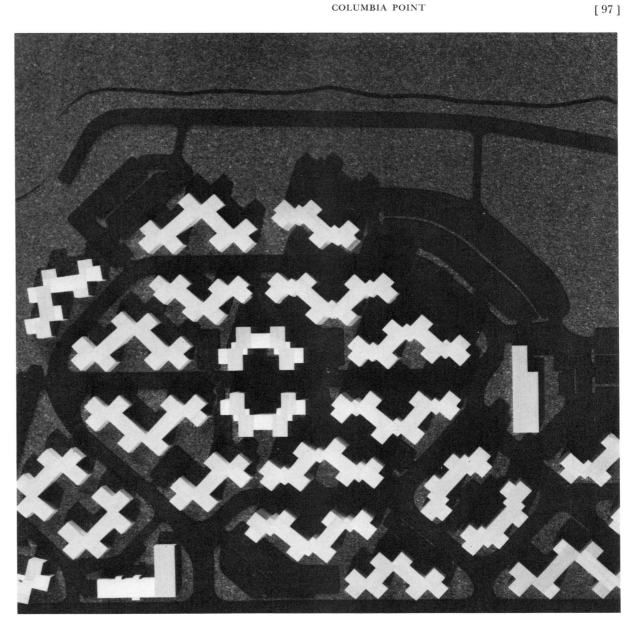

COLUMBIA POINT, Boston
LOCALITY SEGMENT
400 m × 400 m; scale: 1:2500
Model of developed site showing existing buildings and streets

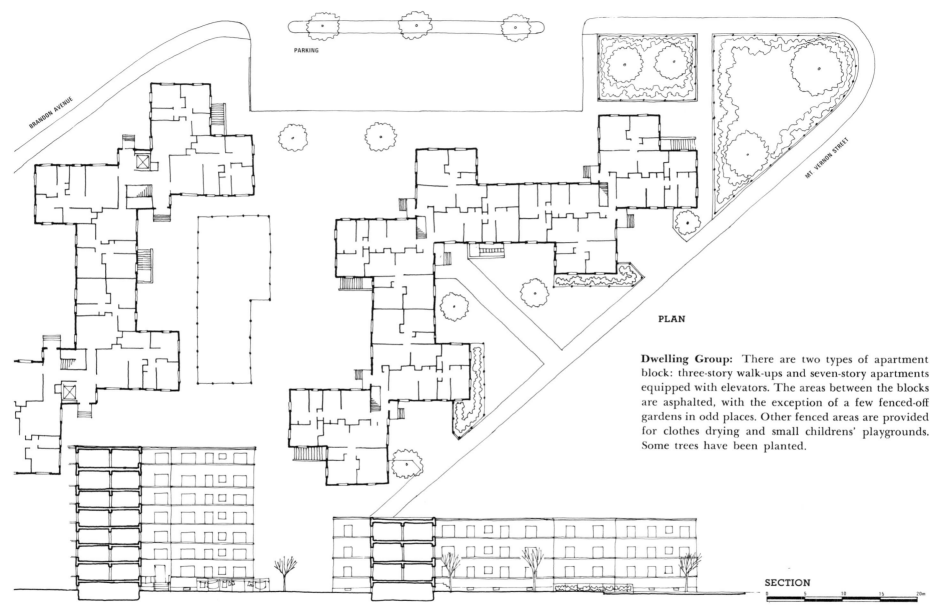

PLAN

Dwelling Group: There are two types of apartment block: three-story walk-ups and seven-story apartments equipped with elevators. The areas between the blocks are asphalted, with the exception of a few fenced-off gardens in odd places. Other fenced areas are provided for clothes drying and small childrens' playgrounds. Some trees have been planted.

SECTION

COLUMBIA POINT, Boston
DWELLING GROUP
Sources: Plans, M. A. Dyer Company, Arch. and Engin., Boston
Quality of information: Accurate

COLUMBIA POINT, Boston Streets, intersection, high-rise apartments. A fenced lawn; a bench; an entrance to an apartment block. (1968)

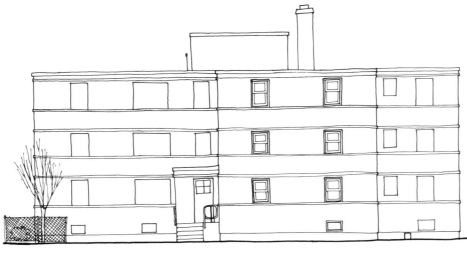

ELEVATION

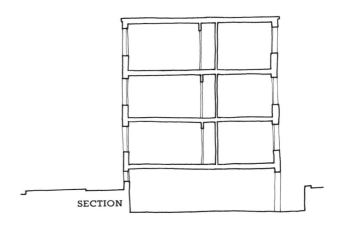

SECTION

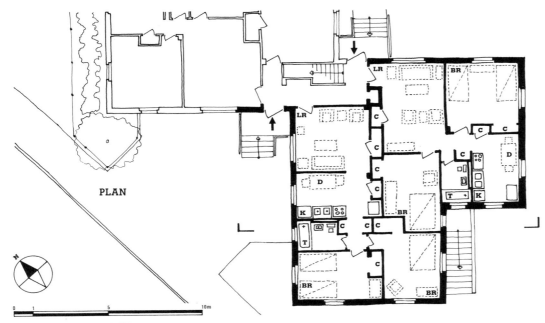

PLAN

N

0 1   5   10m

COLUMBIA POINT, Boston
TYPICAL DWELLING (Public Housing)
Sources: Plans, M. A. Dyer Company, Arch. and Engin.,
    Description of public housing, Castle Square Reloca-
    tion Program, B.R.A.

Quality of information: Approximate

DWELLING-UNIT AREAS

(L-shape unit)	m^2	%
Living (BR, DR, D, LR, K, C)	45.13	57.71
Service (T, L)	7.05	9.02
Circulation	1.44	1.84
Walls	24.58	31.43
Other	—	—
Total Unit Area:	78.20	100.00

Total Lot Area: Not pertinent, public use

LR	Living Room	**K**	Kitchen
DR	Dining Room	**L**	Laundry
D	Dining	**T**	Toilet—Bathroom
BR	Bedroom	**C**	Closet

COLUMBIA POINT, Boston Walk-up apartments in the foreground; high-rise apartments in the background; a fenced lawn; sparsely planted trees with guardrails. (1968)

COLUMBIA POINT, Boston

Dwelling

Design and development: Public housing (government-sponsored; instant development.

Year of construction: 1954.

Type of dwelling: Two-bedroom, walk-up apartment.

Approximate number of people per unit: 4 people.

Approximate dwelling area per person: 19.55 sq. m (L-shaped unit).

Layout: Four apartments served by one stairway; corridors have been minimized, using rooms for circulation; all are exterior rooms; closets are used as a sound buffer between two contiguous apartments; back-to-back kitchen-bathroom plumbing forms a basis for the plan.

Facilities: Minimum kitchen: range, sink, working counter, refrigerator, dining table, storage; bathroom; basement laundry facilities; domestic hot and cold water, central heating and electricity are provided; telephone service is available.

Components: Double hung windows on the four exterior walls.

Type of construction: Masonry walls; reinforced-concrete frame and slab.

For comparison see the following dwellings: East Boston, Charlestown, which are similar public housing projects in Boston.

CAMBRIDGEPORT, Cambridge, Massachusetts, U.S.A.
(Boston Urban Area)

Location: Cambridgeport is a neighborhood of the City of Cambridge, sited on filled marshland in a bend of the Charles River, about 3 kilometers by the most direct route from the central business district of the City of Boston. It is adjacent to the administrative and commercial center of Cambridge and one kilometer from the subcenter at Harvard Square.

Origin: Cambridgeport developed after the opening of the West Boston Bridge in 1793 (later replaced by Longfellow Bridge) and was chartered as a port of entry in 1805. Initially developed more to the north than to the south of Central Square, the area now known as Cambridgeport lies to the south of Central Square, most of which was developed after 1840.

CAMBRIDGEPORT (Boston Urban Area)
LOCALITY PLAN
Sources: Cambridge Planning Board, 1965
Quality of information: Accurate

Layout: Cambridgeport is planned on a regular rectangular grid with the main streets running perpendicular to Massachusetts Avenue, the commercial main circulation spine of Cambridge, or perpendicular to Memorial Drive, the faster traffic route following the Charles River. Three bridges connect Cambridge and Boston through Cambridgeport. The south end of the campus of the Massachusetts Institute of Technology is shown on the plan. (University)

Population: In 1960, the demographic structure of Cambridgeport was similar to that of metropolitan Boston, but it has undoubtedly changed considerably since, if only because of the growing influx of university students. In 1960, the average age of the population was about thirty-six years (as opposed to thirty-one years for the metropolitan area). The total population in 1960 was 3,200 persons, with a slight bias in favor of females (51.5 per cent).

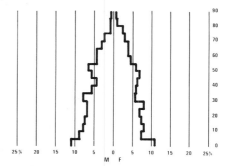

Locality Population Distribution
Census, 1960; tract MC-13; population, 3,200
males: M. 1,552; females: F. 1,648
horizontal: percentages; vertical: ages

CAMBRIDGEPORT (Boston Urban Area) Massachusetts Avenue
at night, head-on meter parking on both sides of the street.

Land Use: Cambridgeport is a heterogeneous area. A large area to the west and a smaller area to the southeast is industrial; the northern side is bordered by the administrative and commercial area of Central Square; and the southern edge is bordered by a riverside park, a school, and a supermarket. Within these borders the area is residential, except for a diminishing number of small commercial enterprises of the neighborhood type—modern traffic patterns and chain-store retailing have all but eliminated the former.

Income Levels: The average income (in 1960) for Cambridgeport was appreciably lower than the metropolitan average: $5,630 per household, per annum, as opposed to $7,440 (but slightly over the average for the lower 80 per cent for Boston, which was $5,500 in 1960).

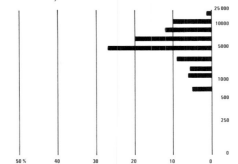

Locality Annual Income Distribution
Census, 1960; tract MC-13; households, 1,307
horizontal: percentages; vertical: dollars

CAMBRIDGEPORT (Boston Urban Area)
LOCALITY LAND-USE PATTERN
Sources: Cambridge Planning Board, 1967
Quality of information: Accurate

H	Health	Bus **(solid line)**	
PO	Post Office	Rapid Transit	
SS	Social Services	**(broken line)**	

Pk	Parking	**Ch**	Church
P	Police	**R**	Recreation
F	Fire Department	**L**	Library
S	School	**U**	University

CAMBRIDGEPORT (Boston Urban Area) Massachusetts Avenue: one of the major commercial ribbon developments in the Boston urban area. Billboard "pop art"; people enjoying a sunny day in the fall; entrance to the subway, Harvard Square-Ashmont line.

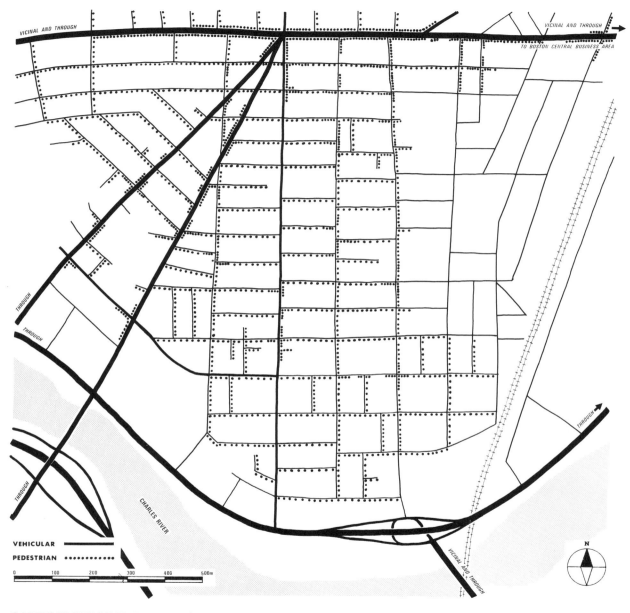

CAMBRIDGEPORT (Boston Urban Area)
LOCALITY CIRCULATION PATTERN
Source: Estimate, B. Creager, 1967
Quality of information: Tentative

Circulation: All streets within Cambridgeport are open to both vehicular and pedestrian traffic; the area between River Street, Memorial Drive, the industrial area, and Massachusetts Avenue is relatively free of fast traffic. This area is also well served by public transport, with an internal, closed-loop bus route in addition to the through bus and subway routes on the adjacent through streets.

The chart illustrates the approximate availability of utilities and services at four levels: no provision at all, very limited or occasional, generally available but inadequate, and adequate or normal service.

Quality of information: Approximate

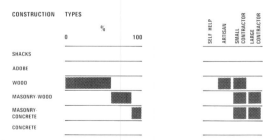

The main dwellings' construction types were grouped as follows: SHACK, ADOBE, WOOD, WOOD AND MASONRY, MASONRY AND CONCRETE, CONCRETE. The main characteristics of these types are described in the introduction.

The building industry was divided into the following groups: SELF-HELP, ARTISAN, SMALL CONTRACTOR, LARGE CONTRACTOR.

The chart shows (1) approximate percentage of each construction type within the total number of dwellings and (2) building group that generally produces each type.

Quality of information: Approximate

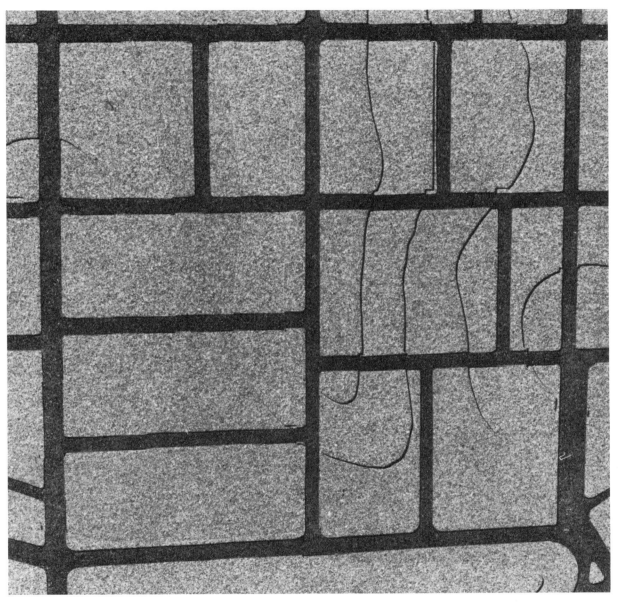

CAMBRIDGEPORT (Boston Urban Area)
LOCALITY SEGMENT
400 m × 400 m; scale: 1:2500
Model of raw site showing topography, main circulation layout

Locality Segment: The typical segment analyzed is almost entirely residential, with 63 per cent of its area occupied by private dwellings. The typical blocks are 73 m × 157 m, with the longer side perpendicular to the principal streets; but there are many exceptions in the segment shown, which has a larger number of smaller blocks of 110 m × 85 m and 110 m × 73 m. Typically, streets are 10 m or 14 m wide.

LOCALITY SEGMENT
AREAS

PRIVATE OWNERSHIP	Hectares	Percentage
Dwelling Lots	10.05	62.81
Commercial	0.15	.94
Industrial	—	—
PUBLIC OWNERSHIP		
Community Centers, Parks Playgrounds, Schools	1.71	10.69
Streets—Parking Pedestrian Walks	4.90	25.56
Total	16.00	100.00

DENSITIES	Number	Hectares	N/Ha
Lots	213	16.00	13.31
Dwelling Units	319	16.00	19.93
Families	319	16.00	19.93
People (4 People/Family)	1276	16.00	79.75

Quality of information: Approximate

CAMBRIDGEPORT (Boston Urban Area)
LOCALITY SEGMENT PLAN
Sources: Cambridge Planning Board, 1965
Quality of information: Accurate

SELECTED BLOCK

AREAS

PRIVATE OWNERSHIP	Hectares	Percentage
Dwelling Lots	0.89	75.42
Commercial	—	—
Industrial	—	—

PUBLIC OWNERSHIP		
Community Center, Parks	—	—
Playground, Schools	—	—
Streets—Parking Pedestrian Walks	0.29	24.58
Total	1.18	100.00

DENSITIES	Number	Hectares	N/Ha
Lots	22	1.18	18.64
Dwelling Units	33	1.18	27.97
Families	33	1.18	27.97
People (4 People/Family)	132	1.18	111.87

CIRCULATION RATIO

$$\frac{\text{Circulation Length} = 230 \text{ m}}{\text{Area} = 1.18 \text{ Ha}} = 195 \text{ m/Ha}$$

Selected block is the area enclosed by the broken line on the Locality Segment plan.

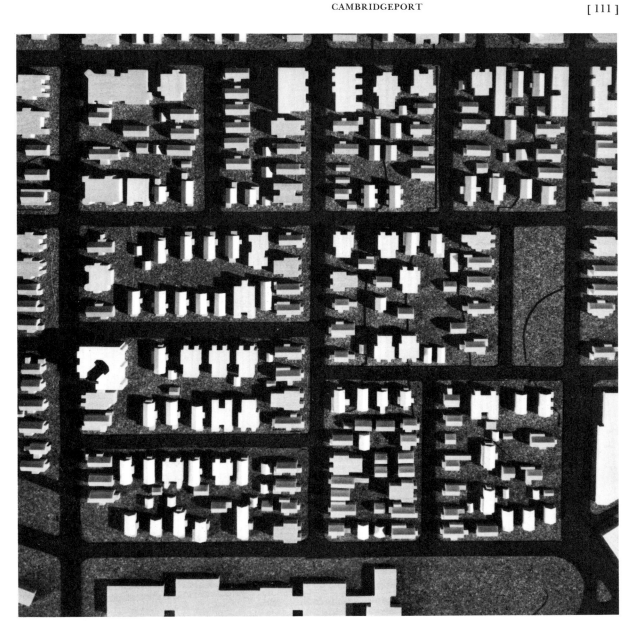

CAMBRIDGEPORT (Boston Urban Area)
LOCALITY SEGMENT
400 m × 400 m; scale: 1:2500
Model of developed site showing existing buildings and streets

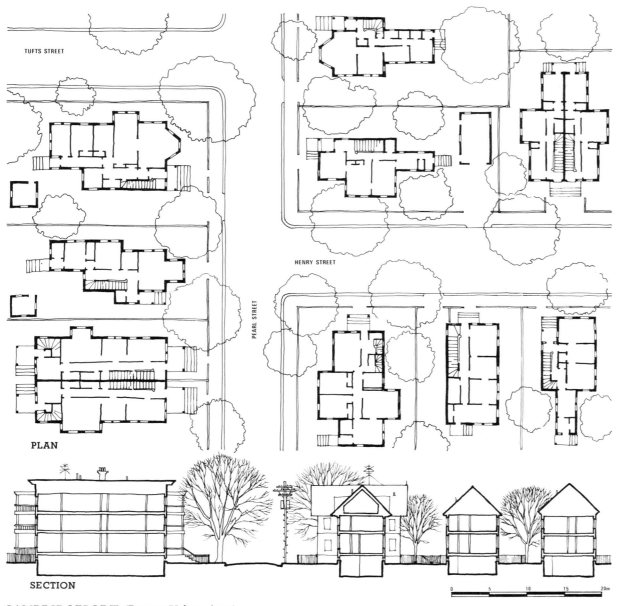

Dwelling Group: Most dwellings in the locality are of timber construction and built between 1840 and 1900. There is a variety of dwelling types in the locality: three- to six-family three-deckers, which are more common near the main through streets, larger and higher-standard apartment buildings; and a large proportion of free-standing single-family houses. The majority of the plots are between 25 m × 32 m deep, but widths vary considerably between 10 m and 30 m. The most common plot size is 14 m × 32 m (450 square meters, approximately).

TUFTS STREET

PEARL STREET

HENRY STREET

PLAN

SECTION

CAMBRIDGEPORT (Boston Urban Area)
DWELLING GROUP
Sources: Inferred from Cambridge Planning Board data, 1965–
          1967
Quality of information: Approximate

CAMBRIDGEPORT (Boston Urban Area) Massachusetts Avenue in the fall. Shops; a typical cinema marquee. (*top right*)

Residential street: balloon-frame multifamily dwellings; electricity and telephone poles and wires. (*top*)

Residential street: balloon-frame multifamily dwellings with distinctive front porches. (*bottom right*)

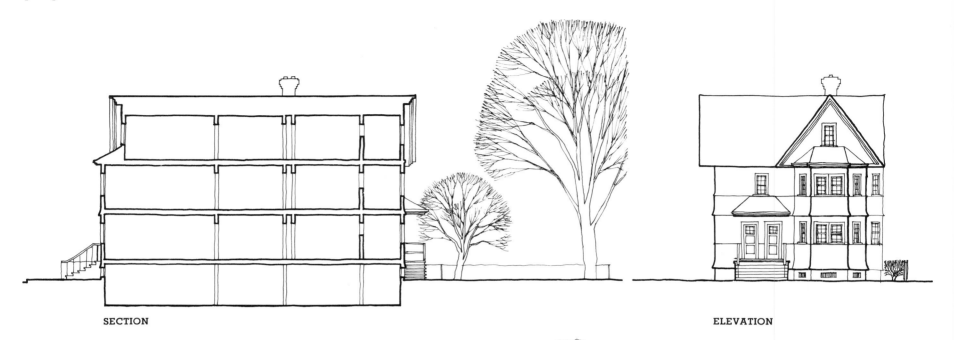

SECTION

ELEVATION

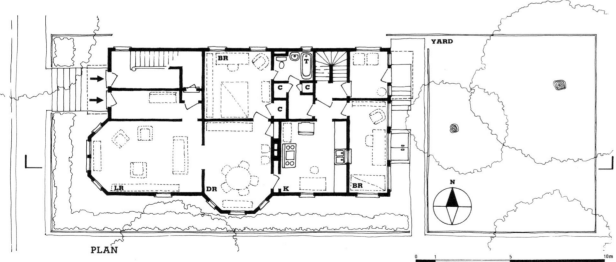

PLAN

YARD

DWELLING-UNIT AREAS

	m^2	%
Living (BR, DR, D, LR, K, C)	75.68	66.27
Service (T, L)	5.19	4.55
Circulation	13.60	11.90
Walls	19.73	17.28
Other	—	—
Total Unit Area:	114.20	100.00

Total Lot Area: 11.00 × 29.00 = 319.00 m², semiprivate use

LR	Living Room	**K**	Kitchen
DR	Dining Room	**L**	Laundry
D	Dining	**T**	Toilet—Bathroom
BR	Bedroom	**C**	Closet

CAMBRIDGEPORT (Boston Urban Area)
TYPICAL DWELLING
Sources: Survey, B. Creager, 1967
Quality of information: Approximate

CAMBRIDGEPORT (Boston Urban Area) A multifamily balloon-frame dwelling. Brick-paved sidewalks are characteristic of many areas in Cambridge and Boston (1968). (*opposite page*)

CAMBRIDGEPORT (Boston Urban Area)

Dwelling

Design and development: Private, instant development.

Year of construction: 1930.

Type of dwelling: Originally a single-family house; presently a two-bedroom, walk-up apartment, detached house.

Approximate number of people per unit: 3 people.

Approximate dwelling area per person: 38.07 sq. m.

Layout: A three-story building with an apartment on each floor very similar to the Washington Park dwelling. But in Washington Park the dwelling was designed and built as an apartment house, whereas in Cambridgeport the original single-family dwelling has been remodeled into apartments. In both cases the building is long and leaves very little open space around. But in the Cambridgeport case, in all probability, the lot was large at the beginning and was subdivided at a later date to provide for other dwellings. Corridors have been minimized by using rooms for circulation—the living room, dining room, kitchen, stair landing, and even the bathroom.

Facilities: A generous kitchen; bathroom; washing and drying machines on unlabeled back room; domestic hot and cold water, central heating; electricity, telephone, as well as limited closet space.

Components: Double hung windows, bay windows in two rooms.

Type of construction: Wooden structure, balloon-frame type.

For comparison see the following dwellings: Washington Park, which is a similar type of dwelling.

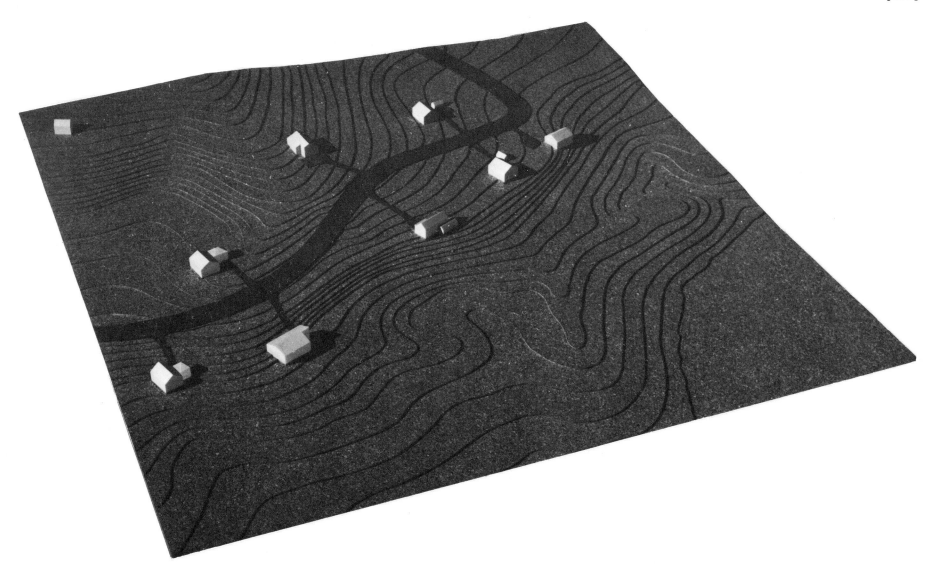

LINCOLN, Massachusetts, U.S.A.
(Boston Urban Area)

Location: Lincoln is a rapidly growing, upper-income suburb, 20 kilometers from the center of Boston, or 45 to 60 minutes by automobile. On wooded, undulating land, mostly too poor for modern agricultural use and studded with ponds, the area is ideal for the high-income commuter.

Origins: The town of Lincoln was incorporated in 1735 and, until the 1930's, had grown very little beyond the relatively compact village center.

Layout: The layout of residential properties (excluding the original village) is determined by the irregular automobile road network that for the most part follows the original pattern of farm tracks. In relation to residential use, the scale is that of the automobile. Since the adoption of zoning in 1929, requirements for minimum lot sizes have increased from 1000 to 8000 square meters (that is, to 2 acres).

Population: The age-sex distribution of Lincoln is similar to those for the peripheral low-income settlements in Peru and Venezuela, a heavy bias toward younger nuclear families. There are very few young adults of college age (20-24). Nearly 70 per cent of the population is composed of adults between the ages of twenty-five to forty-five, and children under fifteen. The over-all population growth rate in 1965 was 3.9 per cent per annum. The 1959 average annual income level was U.S.$10,830, 66 per cent above the metropolitan average. Since that time, the absolute and relative income levels have undoubtedly increased.

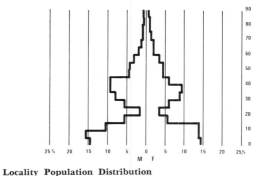

Locality Population Distribution
Census, 1960; tract MC-0133; population, 5,613
males: M. 2,731; females: F. 2,882
horizontal: percentages; vertical: ages

LINCOLN (Boston Urban Area)
LOCALITY PLAN
Sources: Plate 10—Town Map, Planning Board, Lincoln, 1965
Quality of information: Accurate

LINCOLN (Boston Urban Area) Air view. Highway connection; existing and under-contsruction suburban developments; surviving wooded areas. (1968) (*opposite page*)

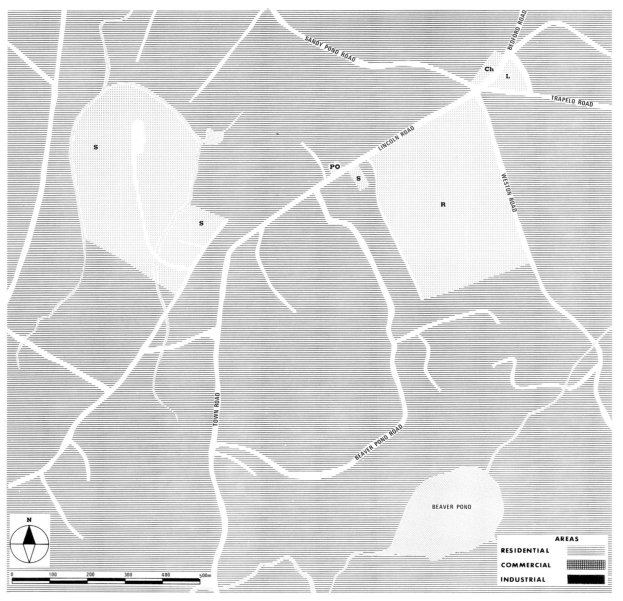

Land Use: The locality is almost exclusively residential but at a very low density. "Lincoln lies within the region predicted to experience the greatest increase in industrial capacity through the 1980's" (State Route 2 passes through the town district).

Incomes: Even in 1960, Lincoln's per capita income was well over three times the national average. It was about forty times the average urban personal income in Peru.

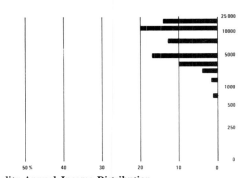

Locality Annual Income Distribution
Census, 1960; tract MC-0133; households, 1,377
horizontal: percentages; vertical: dollars

LINCOLN (Boston Urban Area)
LOCALITY LAND-USE PATTERN
Sources: Comprehensive Development Plan, Town of Lincoln,
    Massachusetts, Adams, Howard, and Oppermann, 1965
Quality of information: Accurate

H	Health	Bus **(solid line)**	**Pk**	Parking	**Ch**	Church
PO	Post Office	Rapid Transit	**P**	Police	**R**	Recreation
SS	Social Services	**(broken line)**	**F**	Fire Department	**L**	Library
			S	School	**U**	University

LINCOLN (Boston Urban Area) Vicinal Lincoln Road: a tunnel in the woods. Lawns run up to the edge of the road. No side walks, no room for pedestrians. (1968)

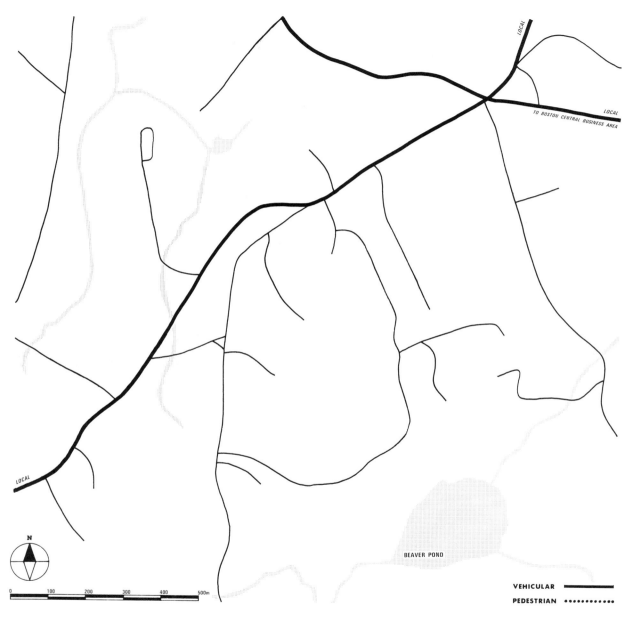

LINCOLN (Boston Urban Area)
LOCALITY CIRCULATION PATTERN
Source: Estimate, B. Cavin, 1967
Quality of information: Approximate

Circulation: The roads are used almost exclusively by automobiles; pedestrian circulation is negligible and is practiced, along with horse riding, more for recreation than for transportation. Nonvehicular tracks and paths exist and are likely to be developed for recreational purposes.

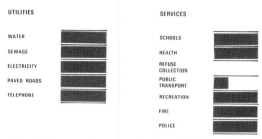

The chart illustrates the approximate availability of utilities and services at four levels: no provision at all, very limited or occasional, generally available but inadequate, and adequate or normal service.

Quality of information: Approximate

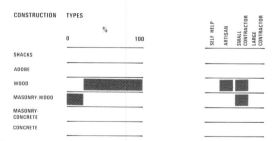

The main dwellings' construction types were grouped as follows: SHACK, ADOBE, WOOD, WOOD AND MASONRY, MASONRY AND CONCRETE, CONCRETE. The main characteristics of these types are described in the introduction.

The building industry was divided into the following groups: SELF-HELP, ARTISAN, SMALL CONTRACTOR, LARGE CONTRACTOR.

The chart shows (1) approximate percentage of each construction type within the total number of dwellings and (2) building group that generally produces each type.

Quality of information: Approximate

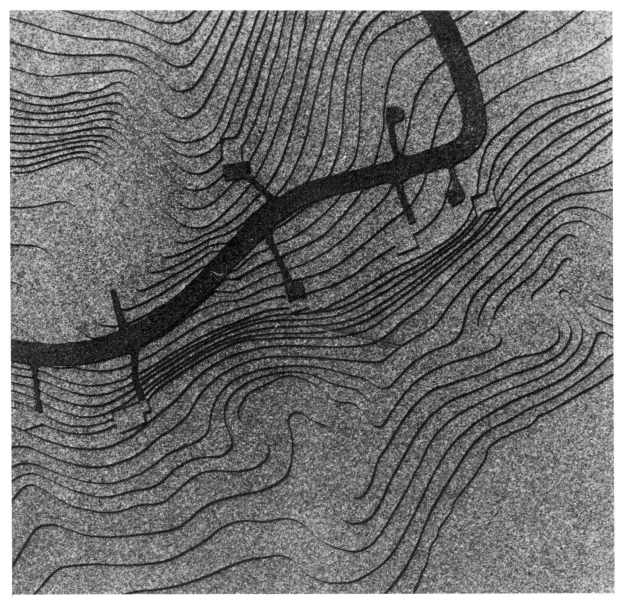

LINCOLN (Boston Urban Area)
LOCALITY SEGMENT
400 m × 400 m; scale: 1:2500
Model of raw site showing topography, main circulation layout

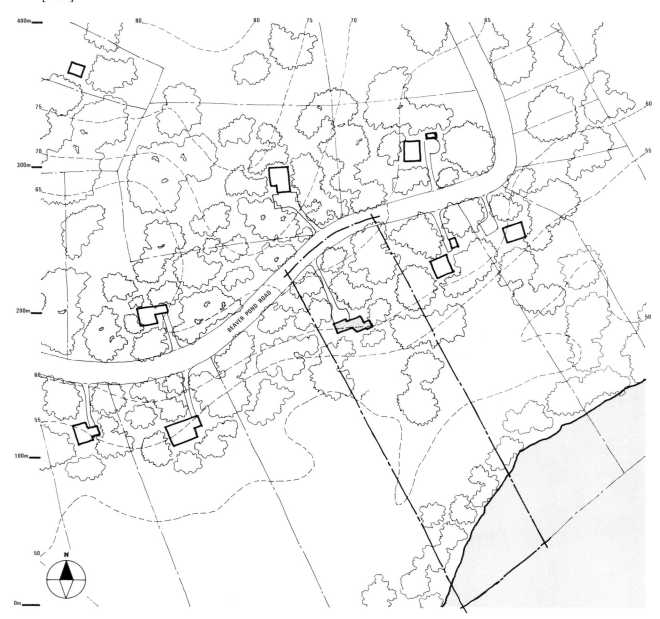

Locality Segment: The residential density of this subdivision is somewhat less than four persons per hectare (one two hundredth of the density of Mendocita, Lima, and over one hundredth for that of Villa Socorro, Medellín, also a single-family dwelling subdivision). Though culturally an entirely urban population, physically Lincoln resembles the primeval forest more than a city.

LOCALITY SEGMENT

AREAS

PRIVATE OWNERSHIP	Hectares	Percentage
Dwelling Lots	15.36	96.00
Commercial	—	—
Industrial	—	—
PUBLIC OWNERSHIP		
Community Centers, Parks	—	—
Playgrounds, Schools	—	—
Streets—Parking	0.64	4.00
Pedestrian Walks	—	—
Total	16.00	100.00

DENSITIES	Number	Hectares	N/Ha
Lots	12	16.00	0.75
Dwelling Units	9	16.00	0.56
Families	9	16.00	0.56
People	36	16.00	2.25
(4 People/Family)			

Quality of information: Approximate

LINCOLN (Boston Urban Area)
LOCALITY SEGMENT PLAN
Sources: Plate 10—Town Map, Planning Board, Lincoln, 1965
Quality of information: Approximate

SELECTED BLOCK

AREAS

PRIVATE OWNERSHIP	Hectares	Percentage
Dwelling Lots	1.70	97.60
Commercial	—	—
Industrial	—	—

PUBLIC OWNERSHIP		
Community Center, Parks	—	—
Playgrounds, Schools	—	—
Streets—Parking Pedestrian Walks	0.04	2.40
Total	1.74	100.00

DENSITIES

	Number	Hectares	N/Ha
Lots	1	1.74	0.57
Dwelling Units	1	1.74	0.57
Families	1	1.74	0.57
People	4	1.74	2.30
(4 People/Family)			

CIRCULATION RATIO

$$\frac{\text{Circulation Length} = 75 \text{ m}}{\text{Area} \quad = 1.74 \text{ Ha}} = 43 \text{ m/Ha}$$

Selected block is the area enclosed by the broken line on the Locality Segment plan.

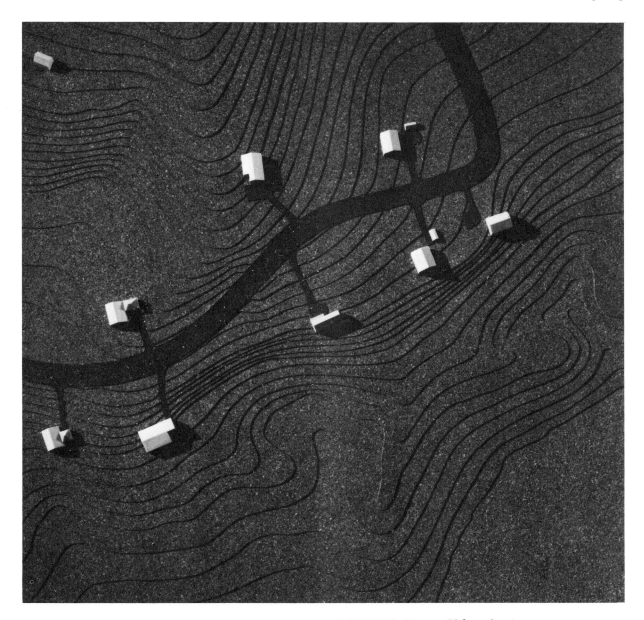

LINCOLN (Boston Urban Area)
LOCALITY SEGMENT
400 m × 400 m; scale: 1:2500
Model of developed site showing existing buildings and streets

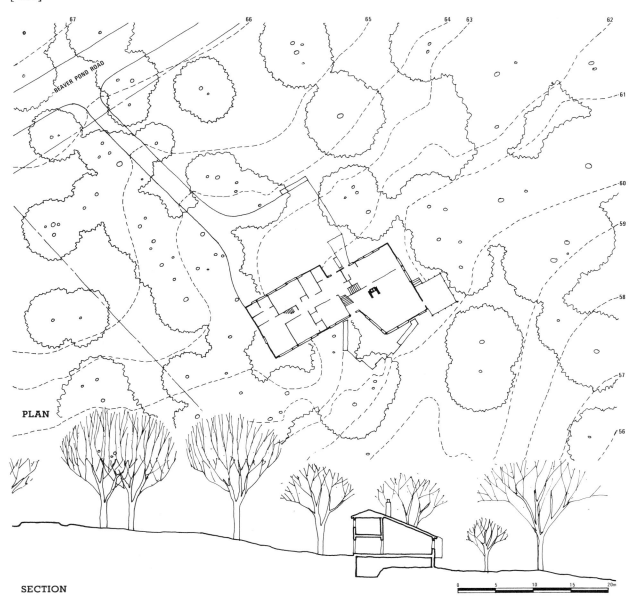

PLAN

SECTION

LINCOLN (Boston Urban Area)
DWELLING GROUP
Sources: Architects Drawings
Quality of information: Accurate

LINCOLN (Boston Urban Area) Air view. Farm dwelling, land plowed following contours, vicinal road, not far from Thoreau's Walden Pond. (1968)

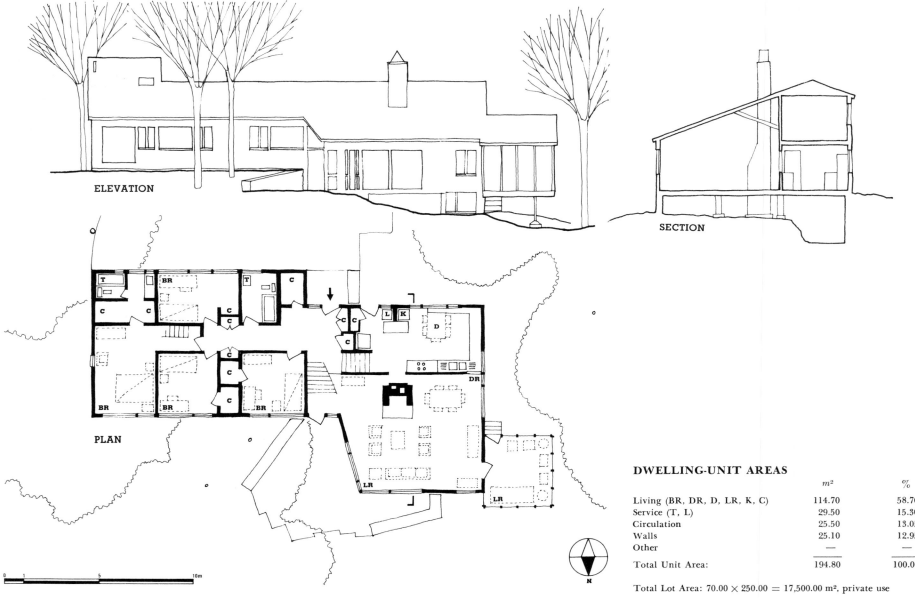

ELEVATION

SECTION

PLAN

DWELLING-UNIT AREAS

	m^2	%
Living (BR, DR, D, LR, K, C)	114.70	58.70
Service (T, L)	29.50	15.30
Circulation	25.50	13.05
Walls	25.10	12.95
Other	—	—
Total Unit Area:	194.80	100.00

Total Lot Area: 70.00 × 250.00 = 17,500.00 m², private use

LR	Living Room	K	Kitchen
DR	Dining Room	L	Laundry
D	Dining	T	Toilet—Bathroom
BR	Bedroom	C	Closet

LINCOLN (Boston Urban Area)
TYPICAL DWELLING
Sources: Architect's drawings
Quality of information: Approximate

N

LINCOLN (Boston Urban Area) Car, dwelling, lawn, pond. The North American dream? (1968)

LINCOLN (Boston Urban Area)

Dwelling

Design and development: Private, tailor-made, instant development.

Year of construction: 1950.

Type of dwelling: Four-bedroom, single-family, detached house.

Approximate number of people per unit: 4 people.

Approximate dwelling area per person: 48.70 sq. m.

Layout: Dwellings in this locality are so well separated that they do not create recognizable "groups" or an intermediate scale between the locality or neighborhood and that of the individual house. Each stands on its own lot, often out of sight of its immediate neighbors. The dwelling illustrated stands in a lot measuring 260 m × 67 m (4 1/3 acres). The dwelling is in a dominant position, and the main rooms are looking toward a panoramic view of woods and a lake; the access to the house is along a private driveway; there is a main and a service entrance.

Facilities: Generous kitchen with approximately 8 m of counter and equipment space; two bathrooms; generous storage space including walk-in closets; a screened porch; a two-car garage with workshop adjacent to the house (not shown in the plan). Domestic hot and cold water, central heating, and telephone services are provided.

Components: Large windows with large pieces of glass face the main views.

Type of construction: Wood frame.

For comparison see the following dwellings: El Agustino (Hill), Villa Socorro, which have similar topography.

CUEVAS, Lima, Peru

Location: The squatter settlement or *barriada* known originally as Pampa de las Cuevas is situated in the re-entrant valley between spurs of the desert Andean foothills, bounded on the west by a highway and an infrequently used railroad bordering irrigated agricultural land. The settlement is 6 kilometers from the central business district of Lima. The land (up to 1965) was a property of the state. Except for the unplanned settlement on the hillsides, the *barriada* is laid out on the relatively flat, sloping floor of the valley formed by the detritus from the decaying hills. These locations enjoy an appreciably higher incidence of sunlight in the winter months than the plain and are also oriented to the prevailing sea-land breeze, a constant feature during the summer months.

Origins: The settlement was established by an organized invasion in December 1960 and gained official recognition as an Urbanizacion Popular the following year. In 1965, Cuevas was incorporated into a newly created municipality, Independencia, by which time it had become a well-established, blue-collar-class residential neighborhood.

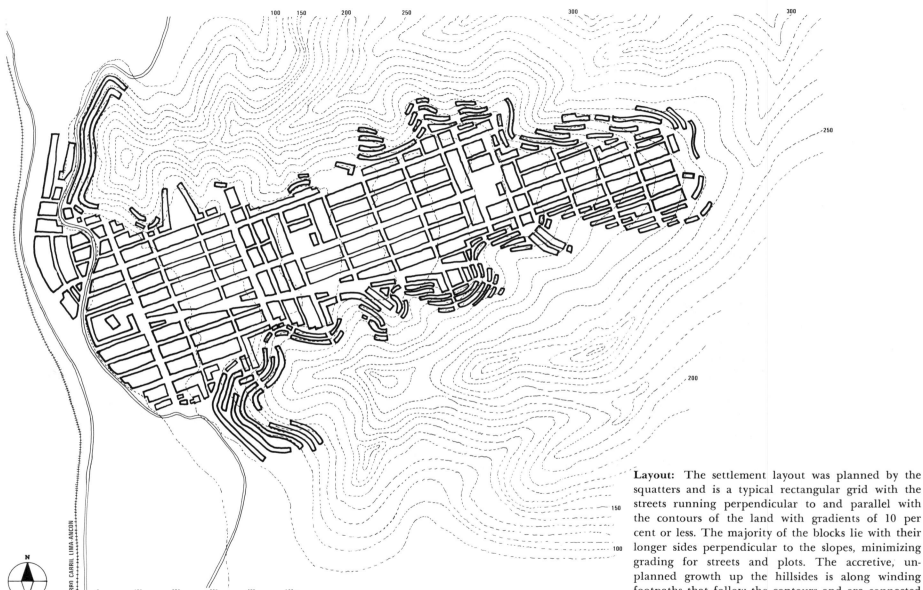

FERRO CARRIL LIMA-ANCON

CUEVAS, Lima
LOCALITY PLAN
Sources: Aerial Photographs 1965; J.N.V., 1962
Quality of information: Accurate

Layout: The settlement layout was planned by the squatters and is a typical rectangular grid with the streets running perpendicular to and parallel with the contours of the land with gradients of 10 per cent or less. The majority of the blocks lie with their longer sides perpendicular to the slopes, minimizing grading for streets and plots. The accretive, unplanned growth up the hillsides is along winding footpaths that follow the contours and are connected by steep paths or stairways perpendicular to the slopes. These have gradients of up to 50 per cent. The total occupied area (in 1965) was approximately 90 hectares, giving a gross density of 133 persons per hectare.

CUEVAS, Lima Air view of the squatter settlement. The rectangular grid of streets runs up to the foot of the hills; the diagonal street is the right of way of a power line existing at the time of the invasion. (1965)

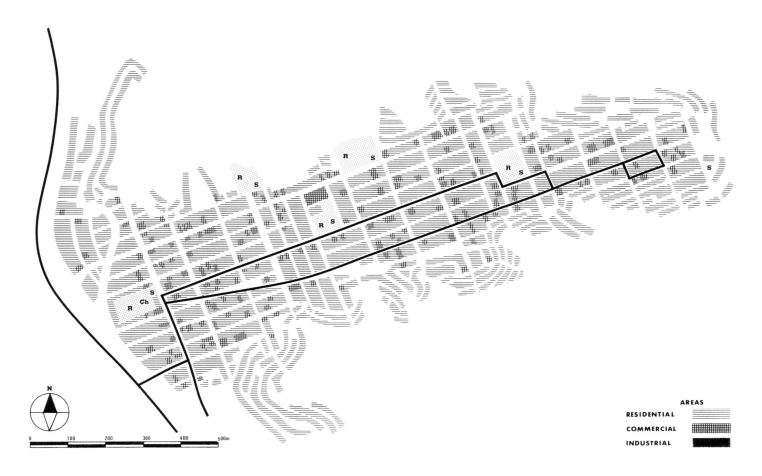

AREAS

RESIDENTIAL

COMMERCIAL

INDUSTRIAL

Land Use: Privately owned dwelling lots occupy exactly two thirds of the built-up area of the settlement, and 8 per cent of these are also used for minor commercial or artisan activities. These are rather evenly distributed throughout the locality with no significant concentration along the main thoroughfares or around the principal open spaces. Two main plazas are provided; near the centrally located plaza there is an open market and, within it, a community building that serves as a church, primary school, and assembly room. There are six primary schools, each of which has some open space adjacent to it.

CUEVAS, Lima
LOCALITY LAND-USE PATTERN
Sources: Pattisson & Chambers Survey, 1955; J.N.V., 1962
Quality of information: Accurate

H	Health	Bus (solid line)
PO	Post Office	Rapid Transit
SS	Social Services	(broken line)

Pk	Parking	Ch	Church
P	Police	R	Recreation
F	Fire Department	L	Library
S	School	U	University

Population: Although settled initially by approximately 300 families, by 1965 there were approximately 2,000 households, mostly young nuclear families, giving a total population of approximately 12,000. The demographic and household characteristics of the Cuevas population is similar to that of El Ermitaño.

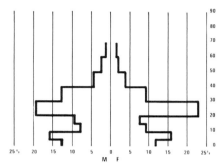

Locality Population Distribution
Survey, El Ermitaño, U.N.S.M., 1965
population sample, 1,493 (equivalent)
males: M. 762; females: F. 731
horizontal: percentages; vertical: ages

Incomes: The average 1965 household income in Cuevas was U.S.$1,030, slightly higher than the average for the metropolitan area and well above the national average.

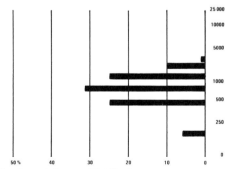

Locality Annual Income Distribution
Survey, U.N.S.M., 1965
horizontal: percentages; vertical: dollars

CUEVAS, Lima Cuevas in the foreground, El Ermitaño in the middle ground; Lima in the background. Sharp definition between the irrigated farm land and the arid urbanized areas. (1963)

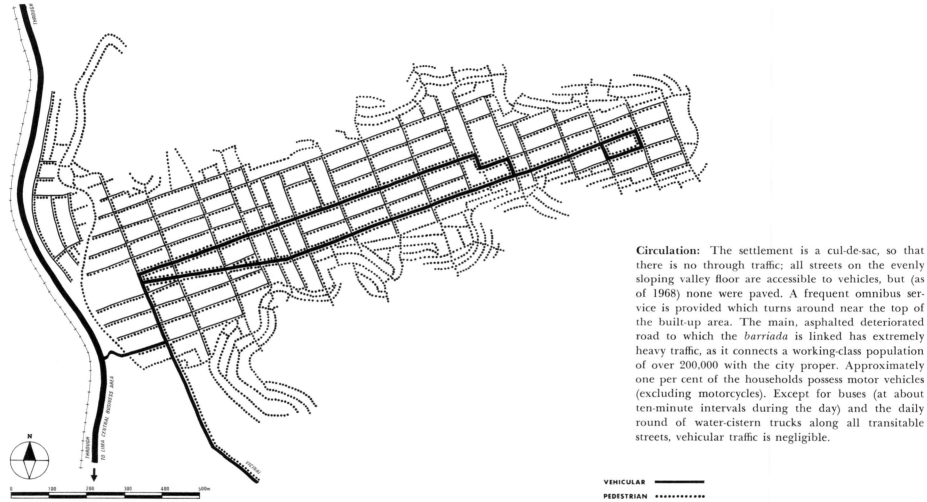

Circulation: The settlement is a cul-de-sac, so that there is no through traffic; all streets on the evenly sloping valley floor are accessible to vehicles, but (as of 1968) none were paved. A frequent omnibus service is provided which turns around near the top of the built-up area. The main, asphalted deteriorated road to which the *barriada* is linked has extremely heavy traffic, as it connects a working-class population of over 200,000 with the city proper. Approximately one per cent of the households possess motor vehicles (excluding motorcycles). Except for buses (at about ten-minute intervals during the day) and the daily round of water-cistern trucks along all transitable streets, vehicular traffic is negligible.

VEHICULAR ▬▬▬▬▬
PEDESTRIAN ●●●●●●●●●●●

CUEVAS, Lima
LOCALITY CIRCULATION PATTERN
Source: Estimate, John F. C. Turner, 1967
Quality of information: Approximate

UTILITIES

WATER

SEWAGE

ELECTRICITY

PAVED ROADS

TELEPHONE

SERVICES

SCHOOLS

HEALTH

REFUSE COLLECTION

PUBLIC TRANSPORT

RECREATION

FIRE

POLICE

The chart illustrates the approximate availability of utilities and services at four levels: no provision at all, very limited or occasional, generally available but inadequate, and adequate or normal service.

Quality of information: Approximate

CONSTRUCTION TYPES

%

0   100

SHACKS

ADOBE

WOOD

MASONRY-WOOD

MASONRY-CONCRETE

CONCRETE

SELF HELP | ARTISAN | SMALL CONTRACTOR | LARGE CONTRACTOR

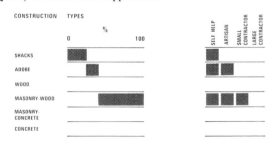

The main dwellings' construction types were grouped as follows: SHACK, ADOBE, WOOD, WOOD AND MASONRY, MASONRY AND CONCRETE, CONCRETE. The main characteristics of these types are described in the introduction.

The building industry was divided into the following groups: SELF-HELP, ARTISAN, SMALL CONTRACTOR, LARGE CONTRACTOR.

The chart shows (1) approximate percentage of each construction type within the total number of dwellings and (2) building group that generally produces each type.

Quality of information: Approximate

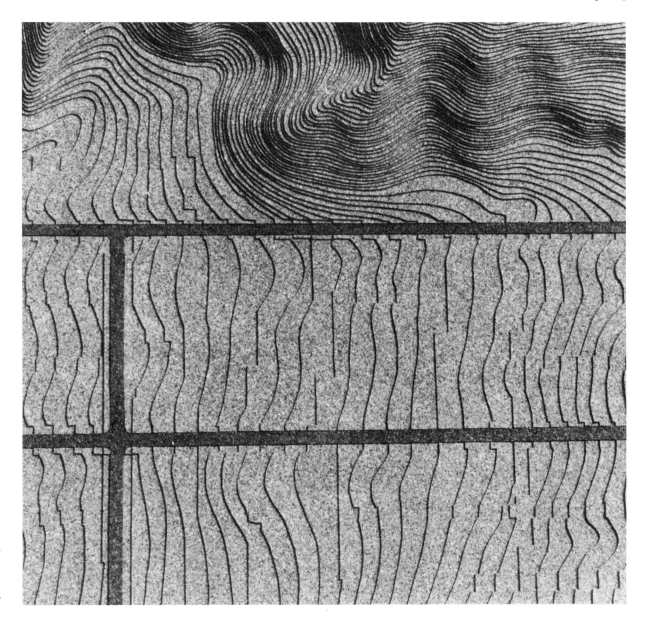

CUEVAS, Lima
LOCALITY SEGMENT
400 m × 400 m; scale: 1:2500
Model of raw site showing topography, main circulation layout

Locality Segment: In the 9.5 hectare area analyzed the approximate density is 30.5 households, or 168 persons per hectare. With the partial exception of the access paths to hillside dwellings, all circulation spaces are fully public and all plots are fully private and, with few exceptions, enclosed from the street. The typical block is 45 m × 100 m and street widths are 10 m, 12 m or 20 m.

LOCALITY SEGMENT

AREAS

PRIVATE OWNERSHIP	Hectares	Percentage
Dwelling Lots	9.50	60.00
Commercial		
Industrial	—	—
PUBLIC OWNERSHIP		
Community Centers, Parks Playgrounds, Schools	3.20	20.00
Streets—Parking Pedestrian Walks	3.30	20.00
Total	16.00	100.00

DENSITIES	Number	Hectares	N/Ha
Lots	488	16.00	30.50
Dwelling Units	488	16.00	30.50
Families	488	16.00	30.50
People (5.5 People/Family)	2684	16.00	167.75

Quality of information: Approximate

CUEVAS, Lima
LOCALITY SEGMENT PLAN
Sources: Photographs, John F. C. Turner, 1964
Quality of information: Approximate

SELECTED BLOCK

AREAS

PRIVATE OWNERSHIP	Hectares	Percentage
Dwelling Lots	0.40	66.67
Commercial		
Industrial	—	—

PUBLIC OWNERSHIP		
Community Center, Parks	—	—
Playgrounds, Schools	—	—
Streets—Parking	0.20	33.33
Pedestrian Walks		
Total	0.60	100.00

DENSITIES	Number	Hectares	N/Ha
Lots	30	0.6	50.00
Dwelling Units	30	0.6	50.00
Families	30	0.6	50.00
People	165	0.6	275.00
(5.5 People/Family)			

CIRCULATION RATIO

$$\frac{\text{Circulation Length} = 180 \text{ m}}{\text{Area} \quad = 0.60 \text{ Ha}} = 300 \text{ m/Ha}$$

Selected block is the area enclosed by the broken line on the Locality Segment plan.

CUEVAS, Lima
LOCALITY SEGMENT
400 m × 400 m; scale: 1:2500
Model of developed site showing existing buildings and streets

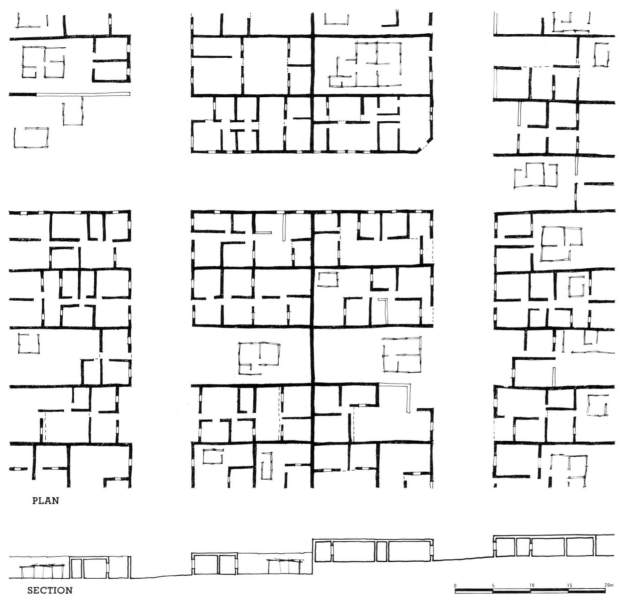

PLAN

SECTION

CUEVAS, Lima
DWELLING GROUP
Sources: Plans interpreted from typical dwellings, Ralph
Pattisson, 1965
Quality of information: Approximate

Dwelling Group: The great majority of individual lots are 8 m × 16 m, and all dwellings are individually built. In 1965, 80 per cent of dwellings were at some stage of permanent construction, 56 per cent had masonry walls of the ground floor completed, and 9 per cent had concrete roofs.

CUEVAS, Lima Group of dwellings in different stages of construction. Walls and fences have a priority over permanent roofs, partly because there is no rainfall in Lima. (1962) (*opposite page*)

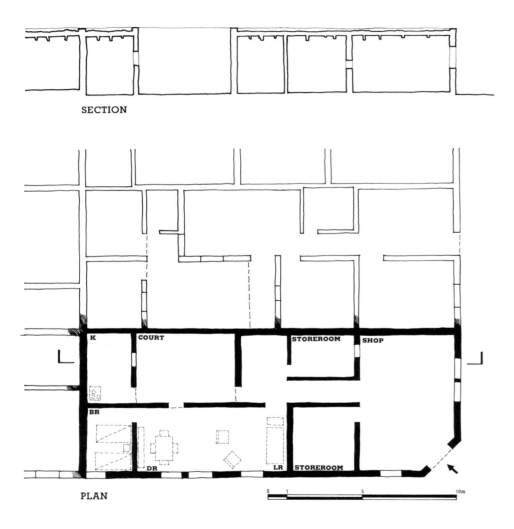

SECTION

ELEVATION

PLAN

DWELLING-UNIT AREAS

	m²	%
Living (BR, DR, D, LR, K, C)	43.00	31.10
Service (T, L)	—	—
Circulation	14.00	9.80
Walls	30.00	21.00
Other (shop, storeroom)	53.00	38.10
Total Unit Area:	140.00	100.00

Total Lot Area: (8.00 × 20.00) − 2.00 = 158.00 m², private use

LR Living Room	**K** Kitchen
DR Dining Room	**L** Laundry
D Dining	**T** Toilet—Bathroom
BR Bedroom	**C** Closet

CUEVAS, Lima
TYPICAL DWELLING
Sources: Ralph Pattisson, 1965
Quality of information: Accurate

CUEVAS, Lima Back court; dwelling; street. Priorities: walls, partitions, fences are completed (using a ceramic brick appropriately called "'King Kong"); only a part of the dwelling is roofed; the front room with a permanent reinforced-concrete slab, the rest with a combination of bamboo canes, mats, and mud. (1962).

CUEVAS, Lima

Dwelling

Design and development: Squatter, progressive development.

Year of construction: 1960 (started).

Type of dwelling: Single-family row house with a shop, corner lot. "Single-family row house" in the *barriada* context means that the individually built houses abut one another; they rarely have structural, party walls.

Approximate number of people per unit: 6 people.

Approximate dwelling area per person: 14.50 sq. m, which does not include shop and storeroom areas.

Layout: The situation in Cuevas is similar to that of the Mariano Melgar dwelling because it is a corner row-house lot and has a shop. But in Cuevas the lot is much smaller, and the "court" becomes a "well" no larger than a room.

Facilities: The kitchen is in one corner of the lot, opening into the court. Of the five Lima localities shown in this survey, the dwellings in Cuevas and El Ermitaño may have a latrine in the backyard; but in El Agustino (Hill and flat) and Mendocita, most of the dwellings do not have such facilities. When this is the case, people use the nearby garbage areas.

Components: See the accompanying photographs and captions.

Type of construction: The average dwelling, when complete, has 100 sq. m of roofed and enclosed space per floor. A second floor may be added later. (In 1965, 65 per cent of the owners declared their intention of adding a second story.) Typically, the dwelling is built by the occupants who contract most of the specialized labor, while the family members, sometimes assisted by relatives or friends, work as laborers. The dwellings are developed in stages, starting with a mat shack in the rear of the lot and, after an approximate average of 15 years, finish up with 100 to 150 sq. m of construction of masonry walls and concrete slab floors. See accompanying photos and captions.

For comparison see the following dwellings: El Ermitaño, which has similar topography; Mariano Melgar, which is a similar corner situation.

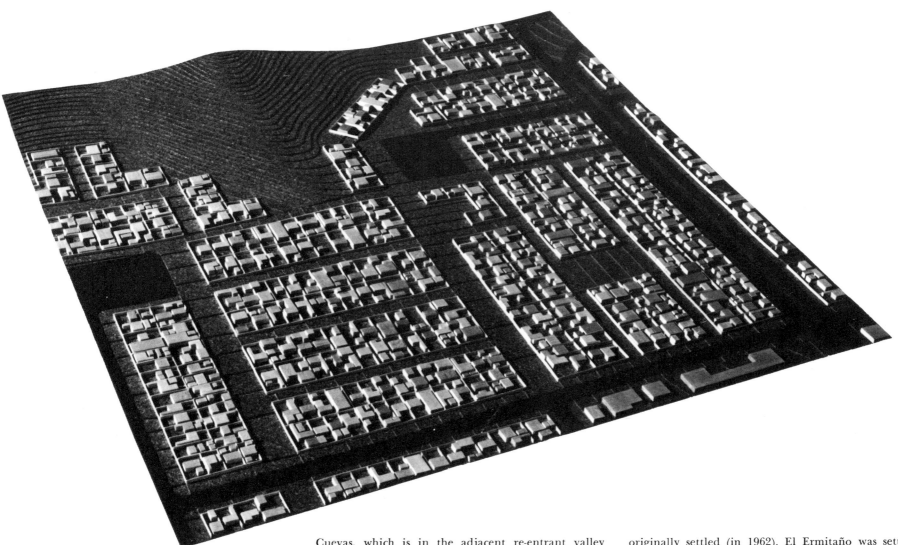

EL ERMITAÑO, Lima, Peru

Location: The squatter settlement or *barriada* Pampa El Ermitaño is situated similarly to Pampa de las Cuevas, which is in the adjacent re-entrant valley and to the north. The center of El Ermitaño is 5 kilometers from the central business district of Lima.

Origins: The land originally occupied by the squatters was state property but was being brought under cultivation by the owner of the adjacent farm land, part of which was appropriated by the government to allow for replanning and extension of the area originally settled (in 1962). El Ermitaño was settled initially in the same way as Cuevas—by the pre-planned organized invasion of several hundred families, in May 1962. The following year the settlement was recognized as an *urbanizacion popular,* and the government housing agency undertook the physical replanning of the settlement. In 1965, El Ermitaño became part of the newly created municipal district of Independencia.

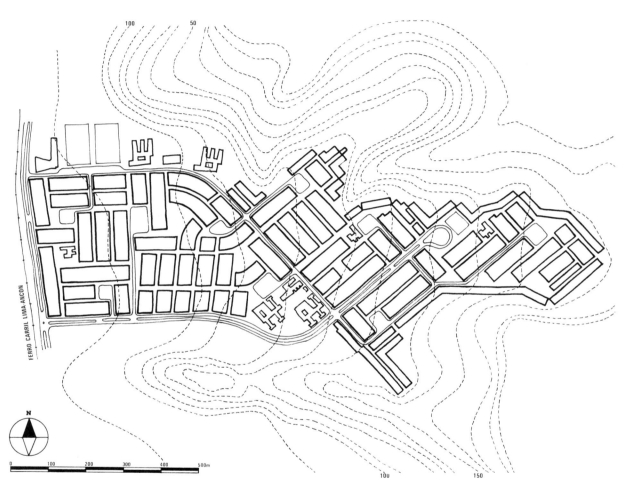

Layout: The present layout was designed by the National Housing Agency (Junta Nacional de la Vivienda) with the exception of a group of ten blocks, the only area planned and allocated by the squatters who were unable to continue successfully (as in Pampa de las Cuevas) owing to excess population. After acquiring this additional land, the housing agency reallocated plots on a plan in which the streets run diagonally across the slopes; this reduces the gradient of the main streets but increases the grading required for the lots. Like Cuevas, El Ermitaño has planned accretive growth on the hillsides.

Population: As shown in the age-sex pyramid, the population is roughly balanced, with a slight preponderance of young, adult females and of older adult males. There are few youths or adolescents, indicating a high proportion of young nuclear families (in which the mothers are generally younger than the fathers).

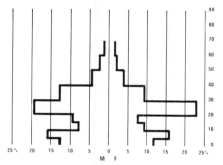

Locality Population Distribution
U.N.S.M. survey, 1965; population sample, 1,493
males: M. 762; females: F. 731
horizontal: percentages; vertical: ages

EL ERMITAÑO, Lima
LOCALITY PLAN
Sources: J.N.V., 1964
Quality of information: Accurate

EL ERMITAÑO, Lima This air view of El Ermitaño shows a setting similar to Cuevas but a different layout. The settlement layout in Cuevas was planned by the squatters. The area of El Ermitaño invaded (the desert land above the irrigation ditch) was overcrowded; the squatter's attempt to plan the area was paralyzed when it became apparent that there was insuffi-cient land to provide adequate plots for all. Except for the group of 10 more-developed blocks, the area was planned by the government agency that expropriated the previously cultivated area between the irrigation ditch and the road; this was done in order to provide all resident families with adequate plots, but as the unplanned growth on the hillsides show, the new area was insufficient. Cuevas layout is straightforward, takes full advantage of the slope, and provides a simple system of circulation. El Ermitaño layout is wasteful, makes bad use of the slopes, and creates a chaotic circulation. (1965)

Land Use: Local commerce is more concentrated than in Cuevas, especially in the blocks laid out by the squatters which have been occupied continually by the same households. A higher proportion of open space is provided than in Cuevas. Schools are concentrated in three locations, two of which are provided with relatively generous play areas. There is a football pitch in the northwest corner, a recreation area shared with Cuevas, in which a community and parochial center is located, financed by private charities and government agencies.

Incomes: The average household income in 1965 was U.S.$595; this is above the national average but 12.5 per cent below the average for Lima.

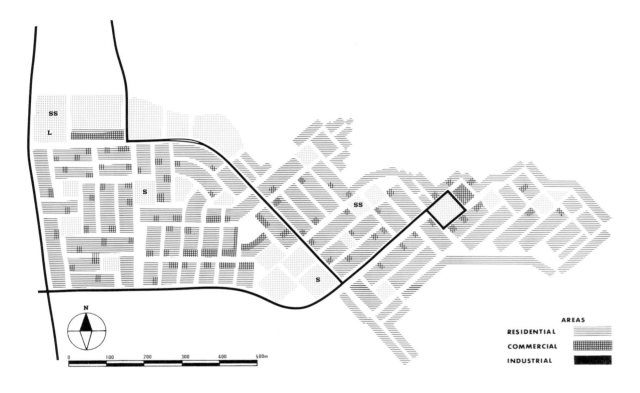

AREAS

RESIDENTIAL

COMMERCIAL

INDUSTRIAL

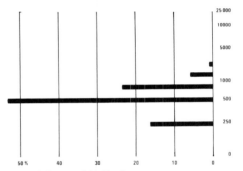

Locality Annual Income Distribution
U.N.S.M. survey, 1965; households, 421
horizontal: percentages; vertical: dollars

EL ERMITAÑO, Lima Air view; farm land in the foreground; El Ermitano in the middle ground; Cuevas in the background. Here again, the irrigated farm land is in sharp contrast with the land lacking water: the urbanized areas and the barren mountains. (1962) (*opposite page*)

EL ERMITAÑO, Lima
LOCALITY LAND-USE PATTERN
Sources: Inferred from Cuevas data, J.C.U.S.
Quality of information: Tentative

H   Health   Bus (**solid line**)
PO Post Office   Rapid Transit
SS Social Services (**broken line**)

Pk Parking   **Ch** Church
P   Police   **R**   Recreation
F   Fire Department **L** Library
S   School   **U**   University

Circulation: Like Cuevas, the settlement is a cul-de-sac with no through traffic; though all planned streets are accessible to vehicular traffic, none were paved in 1965. Except for buses and trucks, vehicular traffic is negligible. A frequent omnibus service is provided by several independent, privately owned companies, one of which runs its buses to the head of the settled area. El Ermitaño is linked to the same very busy main road as Cuevas.

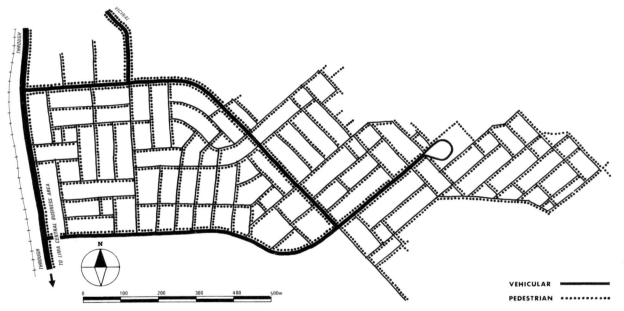

The chart illustrates the approximate availability of utilities and services at four levels: no provision at all, very limited or occasional, generally available but inadequate, and adequate or normal service.

Quality of information: Approximate

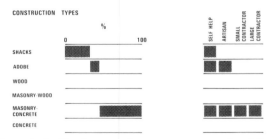

The main dwellings' construction types were grouped as follows: SHACK, ADOBE, WOOD, WOOD AND MASONRY, MASONRY AND CONCRETE, CONCRETE. The main characteristics of these types are described in the introduction.

The building industry was divided into the following groups: SELF-HELP, ARTISAN, SMALL CONTRACTOR, LARGE CONTRACTOR.

The chart shows (1) approximate percentage of each construction type within the total number of dwellings and (2) building group that generally produces each type.

Quality of information: Approximate

VEHICULAR ━━━━━
PEDESTRIAN ••••••••••••

EL ERMITAÑO, Lima
LOCALITY CIRCULATION PATTERN
Source: Estimate, John F. C. Turner, 1967
Quality of information: Approximate

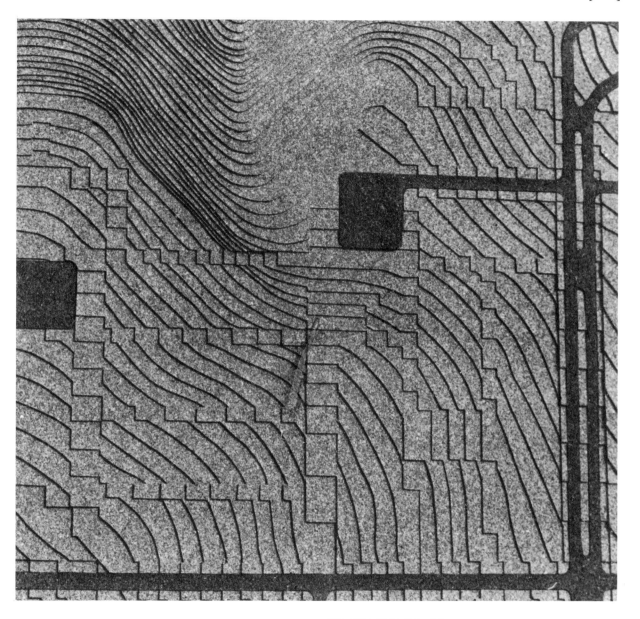

EL ERMITAÑO, Lima
LOCALITY SEGMENT
400 m × 400 m; scale: 1:2500
Model of raw site showing topography, main circulation layout

Locality Segment: In the 6.8-hectare area analyzed the density is approximately 165 persons per hectare. As in Cuevas, and unlike Mendocita or El Agustino, there are no "semipublic" courts or passageways—property is either fully public or private. The typical block is 125 m × 40 m, but there are a dozen that are appreciably longer (up to 200 m). Streets are 10 m, 12 m, 20 m, and 30 m wide—the majority being 10 m and 20 m.

LOCALITY SEGMENT

AREAS

PRIVATE OWNERSHIP	Hectares	Percentage
Dwelling Lots		
Commercial	6.80	42.50
Industrial	—	—
PUBLIC OWNERSHIP		
Community Center, Parks		
Playground, Schools	2.61	16.31
Streets—Parking	1.74	10.88
Pedestrian Walks	4.85	30.31
Total	16.00	100.00

DENSITIES	Number	Hectares	N/Ha
Lots	417	16.00	26.06
Dwelling Units	417	16.00	26.06
Families	417	16.00	26.06
People	2294	16.00	143.38
(5.5 People/Family)			

Quality of information: Approximate

EL ERMITAÑO, Lima
LOCALITY SEGMENT PLAN
Sources: J.N.V., 1964
Quality of information: Accurate

SELECTED BLOCK

AREAS

PRIVATE OWNERSHIP	Hectares	Percentage
Dwelling Lots Commercial	1.68	61.09
Industrial	—	—
PUBLIC OWNERSHIP		
Community Center, Parks	—	—
Playground, Schools	—	—
Streets—Parking	0.32	11.65
Pedestrian Walks	0.75	30.31
Total	2.75	100.00

DENSITIES	Number	Hectares	N/Ha
Lots	104	2.75	37.82
Dwelling Units	104	2.75	37.82
Families	104	2.75	37.82
People	572	2.75	208.00
(5.5 People/Family)			

CIRCULATION RATIO

$$\frac{\text{Circulation Length} = 720 \text{ m}}{\text{Area} \quad\quad = 2.75 \text{ Ha}} = 262 \text{ m/Ha}$$

Selected block is the area enclosed by the broken line on the Locality Segment plan.

EL ERMITAÑO, Lima
LOCALITY SEGMENT
400 m × 400 m; scale: 1:2500
Model of developed site showing existing buildings and streets

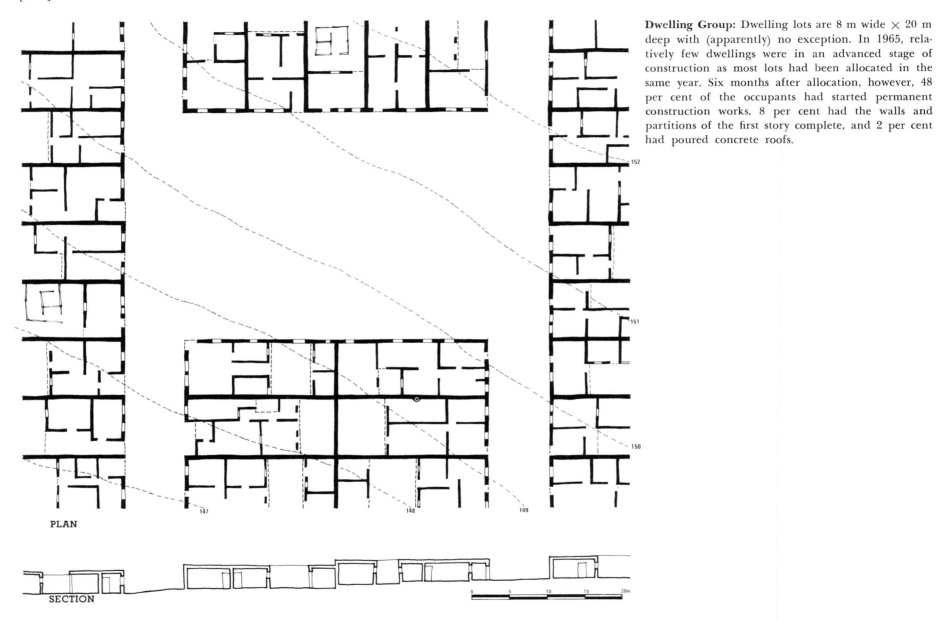

PLAN

SECTION

Dwelling Group: Dwelling lots are 8 m wide × 20 m deep with (apparently) no exception. In 1965, relatively few dwellings were in an advanced stage of construction as most lots had been allocated in the same year. Six months after allocation, however, 48 per cent of the occupants had started permanent construction works, 8 per cent had the walls and partitions of the first story complete, and 2 per cent had poured concrete roofs.

EL ERMITAÑO, Lima
DWELLING GROUP
Sources: Inferred from typical dwellings, Ralph Pattisson, 1965
Quality of information: Approximate

EL ERMITAÑO, Lima An air view showing part of the area planned by the squatters (in the foreground). Internal conflicts arising out of the overpopulation of the area prevented the completion of this operation. (1962) (*opposite page*)

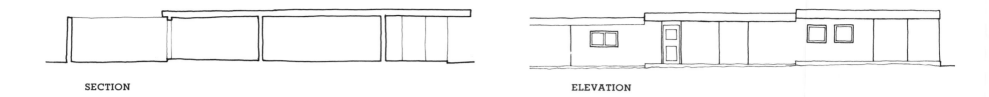

SECTION

ELEVATION

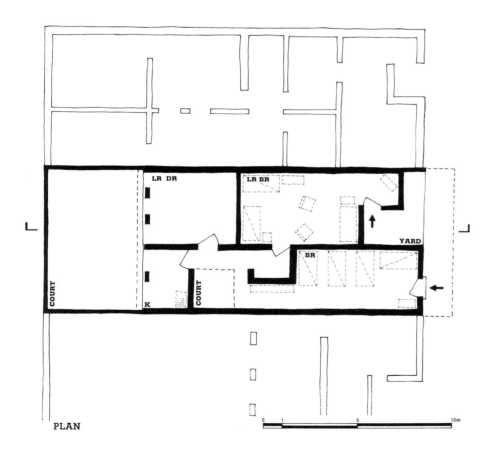

PLAN

EL ERMITAÑO, Lima
TYPICAL DWELLING
Sources: Urbanizacion Popular: Lima 1965, Ralph Pattisson, 1967
Quality of information: Accurate

DWELLING-UNIT AREAS

	m²	%
Living (BR, DR, D, LR, K, C)	73.00	66.00
Service (T, L)	—	—
Circulation	10.00	9.00
Walls	27.00	25.00
Other	—	—
Total Unit Area:	110.00	100.00

Total Lot Area: 8.00 × 20.00 = 160.00 m², semiprivate use

LR	Living Room	**K**	Kitchen
DR	Dining Room	**L**	Laundry
D	Dining	**T**	Toilet—Bathroom
BR	Bedroom	**C**	Closet

EL ERMITAÑO, Lima Dwelling court; children, straw mats for walls and floor. Barrels are for storage of water that is supplied to the locality by trucks.

EL ERMITAÑO, Lima

Dwelling

Design and development: Squatter, progressive development.

Year of construction: 1962 (started).

Type of dwelling: Two-family row house. "Single-family row house" in the *barriada* context means that the individually built houses abut one another; they rarely have structural, party walls.

Approximate number of people per unit: 10 people.

Approximate dwelling area per person: 11.00 sq. m.

Layout: The dwelling is divided in two for the purpose of renting; two independent entrances are provided, but there is only one kitchen which is in the open back court probably shared by the tenant and owner; there are no corridors, rooms are used for circulation.

Facilities: No toilets; some of the dwellings have a latrine in the backyard; otherwise people use garbage areas.

Components: There are no windows; exterior door openings are used to provide daylight and ventilation.

Type of construction: Masonry bearing walls of "king kong" bricks are used with reinforced-concrete piers and reinforced-concrete roof slabs.

For comparison see the following dwellings: Cuevas, which has a similar topography; El Agustino (Flat, hill), Mariano Melgar, which are other types of squatters' row housing.

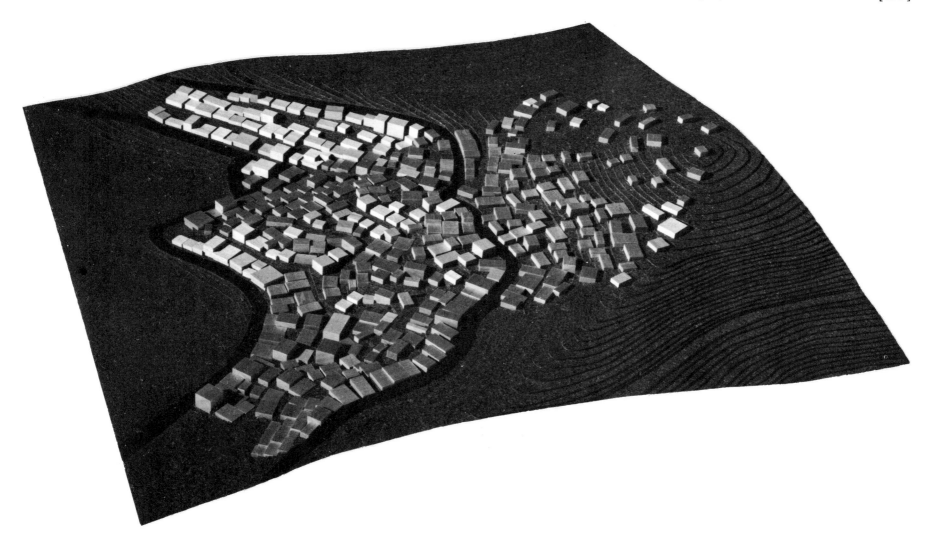

EL AGUSTINO (Hill), Lima, Peru

Location: The *barriada* Cerro El Agustino is located on the hillsides and spurs enclosing *Zona* 26 or El Agustino (flat). The gradients vary between 20 per cent and 40 per cent, and the surface is decayed rock. Being desert, the land was property of the state.

Origins: The *barriada* was established in 1947 by a small number of families who, despite police harass-ment, settled the lower edge of the hillside. It has grown continuously by accretion since that time, the newest settlers occupying cane-matting shacks high up on the slope. Many of the older dwellings on the lower slopes are relatively large, permanent structures and many have two stories.

EL AGUSTINO (Hill), Lima
LOCALITY PLAN
Sources: Servicio Aerofotográfico Nacional, Peru, 1961–1965
Quality of information: Accurate

Layout: While there is a clear structure to the subdivision, with streets mainly parallel to the contours and passages, many with stairways running perpendicular to them, there was evidently no attempt at preplanning the entire area. It appears to have grown by the accretion of the individual or small-group decisions.

Population: The approximate population in 1964–1965 was around 2,500 persons in some 460 households with an (assumed) average of 5.5. On the assumption that the demographic characteristics of El Agustino for 1965 were similar to those of an earlier but similar neighboring *barriada* (San Cosme) in 1961, the average age of the El Agustino inhabitants in 1965 would have been sixteen years (as against fourteen years in El Ermitaño and twenty-one years in metropolitan Lima).

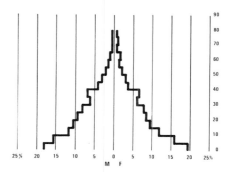

Locality Population Distribution
Survey, San Cosme, J.N.V., 1961 (equivalent)
males: M. ———; females: F. ———
horizontal: percentages; vertical: ages

EL AGUSTINO (Hill and Flat), Lima Air view of the two localities. Winding roads mark the ridge and the base of the hill. Strips of dwellings follow contours. (1957) (*opposite page*)

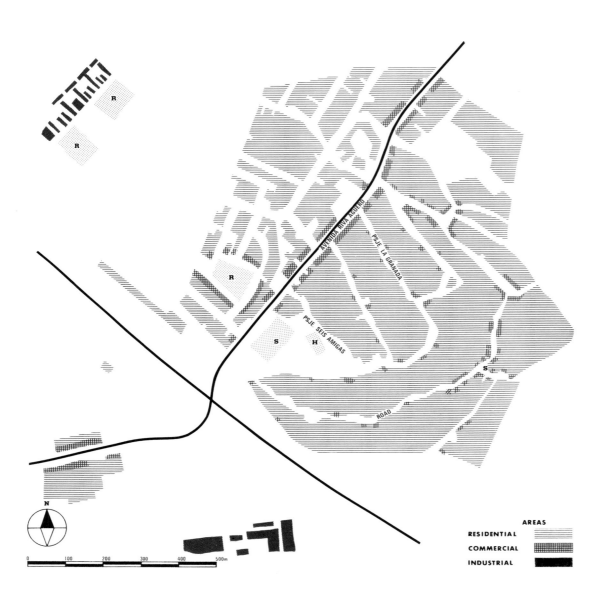

EL AGUSTINO (Hill, Flat), Lima
LOCALITY LAND-USE PATTERN
Sources: Servicio Aerofotográfico Nacional, Peru, 1961–1965
Quality of information: Approximate

H	Health	**Bus (solid line)**	
PO	Post Office	Rapid Transit	
SS	Social Services	**(broken line)**	

Pk	Parking	**Ch**	Church
P	Police	**R**	Recreation
F	Fire Department	**L**	Library
S	School	**U**	University

AREAS

RESIDENTIAL

COMMERCIAL

INDUSTRIAL

Land Use: Privately occupied land accounts for approximately 73 per cent of the land surface; petty commercial activities are scattered along the principal road, and a few are located on pedestrian passageways. There are some cul-de-sacs and internal courtyards giving access to several plots that would be regarded as private to the immediate neighbors; generally the land surface is clearly divided into private and public areas in the built-up portions. There is only one school in the area and no open spaces except for the roads and passages.

Incomes: No data are available on personal incomes for this locality.

EL AGUSTINO (Hill), Lima Panoramic air view: mountains, farm land, squatters. At the foot of the hill continuous rows of dwellings show an advanced stage of development. Toward the top of the hill, scattered dwellings show initial stages. (1962) (*opposite page*)

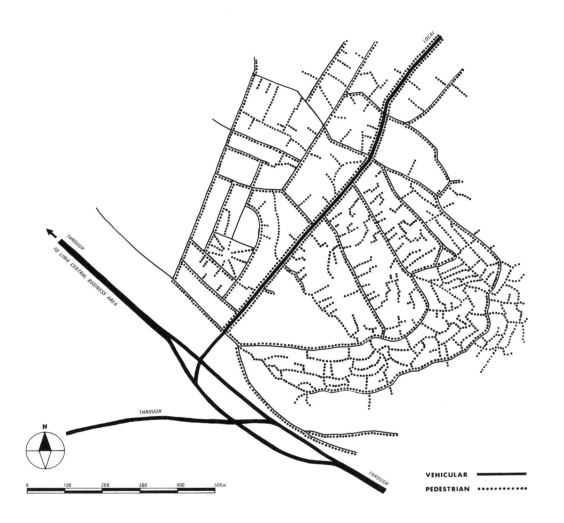

VEHICULAR ▬▬▬▬
PEDESTRIAN •••••••••••

scale: 0 100 200 300 400 500m

EL AGUSTINO (Flat, Hill), Lima
LOCALITY CIRCULATION PATTERN
Source: Estimate, John F. C. Turner, 1967
Quality of information: Approximate

Circulation: The *barriada* has only one vehicular road passing through the settlement and connecting it with the adjacent *barriadas* (San Pedro and Siete de Octubre) and the main roads. The other passageways are for pedestrian use only, the principal paths running parallel to the contours and the narrower, connecting passages perpendicular to them and with concrete stairways on the steeper slopes.

UTILITIES   SERVICES

WATER   SCHOOLS
SEWAGE   HEALTH
ELECTRICITY   REFUSE COLLECTION
PAVED ROADS   PUBLIC TRANSPORT
TELEPHONE   RECREATION
                             FIRE
                             POLICE

The chart illustrates the approximate availability of utilities and services at four levels: no provision at all, very limited or occasional, generally available but inadequate, and adequate or normal service.

Quality of information: Approximate

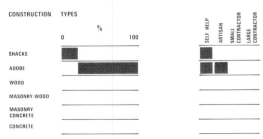

CONSTRUCTION TYPES

SHACKS
ADOBE
WOOD
MASONRY-WOOD
MASONRY-CONCRETE
CONCRETE

The main dwellings' construction types were grouped as follows: SHACK, ADOBE, WOOD, WOOD AND MASONRY, MASONRY AND CONCRETE, CONCRETE. The main characteristics of these types are described in the introduction.

The building industry was divided into the following groups: SELF-HELP, ARTISAN, SMALL CONTRACTOR, LARGE CONTRACTOR.

The chart shows (1) approximate percentage of each construction type within the total number of dwellings and (2) building group that generally produces each type.

Quality of information: Approximate

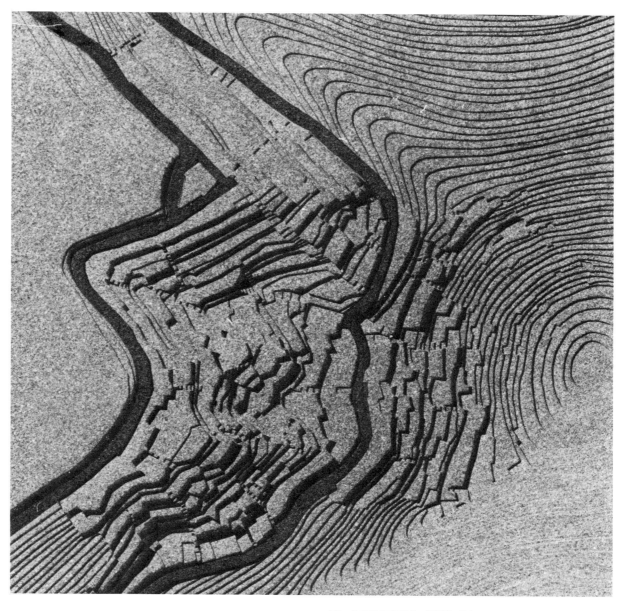

EL AGUSTINO (Hill), Lima
LOCALITY SEGMENT
400 m × 400 m; scale: 1:2500
Model of raw site showing topography, main circulation layout

Locality Segment: In the plan of the locality segment the complete or near-complete structures are outlined in one swathe of the slope; the higher density of permanent structures near the vehicular roads can be appreciated as well as the very much lower density of permanent building in the most recent (and highest) area.

LOCALITY SEGMENT

AREAS

PRIVATE OWNERSHIP	Hectares	Percentage
Dwelling Lots		
Commercial	5.11	75.59
Industrial	—	—
PUBLIC OWNERSHIP		
Community Centers, Parks	—	—
Playgrounds, Schools	—	—
Streets—Parking	0.52	7.69
Pedestrian Walks	1.13	16.72
Total	6.76	100.00

DENSITIES	Number	Hectares	N/Ha
Lots	460	6.76	68.05
Dwelling Units	460	6.76	68.05
Families	460	6.76	68.05
People	2530	6.76	374.26
(5.5 People/Family)			

Quality of information: Approximate

EL AGUSTINO (Hill), Lima
LOCALITY SEGMENT PLAN
Sources: Servicio Aerofotográfico Nacional, Peru, 1961–1965
Quality of information: Approximate

SELECTED BLOCK

AREAS

PRIVATE OWNERSHIP	Hectares	Percentage
Dwelling Lots		
Commercial	1.78	72.95
Industrial	—	—

PUBLIC OWNERSHIP		
Community Center, Parks	—	—
Playground, Schools	—	—
Streets—Parking	0.22	9.02
Pedestrian Walks	0.44	18.03
Total	2.44	100.00

DENSITIES	Number	Hectares	N/Ha
Lots	179	2.44	73.36
Dwelling Units	179	2.44	73.37
Families	179	2.44	73.37
People	984	2.44	403.28
(5.5 People/Family)			

CIRCULATION RATIO

$$\frac{\text{Circulation Length} = 1670 \text{ m}}{\text{Area} \qquad = 2.44 \text{ Ha}} = 644 \text{ m/Ha}$$

Selected block is the area enclosed by the broken line on the Locality Segment plan.

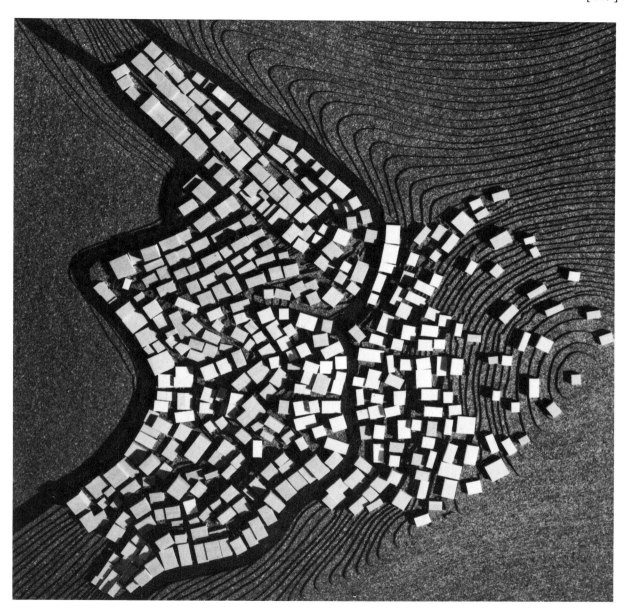

EL AGUSTINO (Hill), Lima
LOCALITY SEGMENT
400 m × 400 m; scale: 1:2500
Model of developed site showing existing buildings and streets

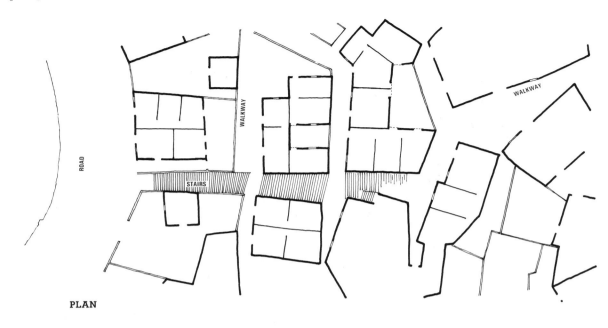

PLAN

Dwelling Group: While the plots are irregular in shape and vary considerably in area, they are generally larger than those in El Agustino (flat), and owing to the considerable gradient the effective area is greater. Of greater significance is the use of the slope to increase daylight, ventilation, and access from different levels.

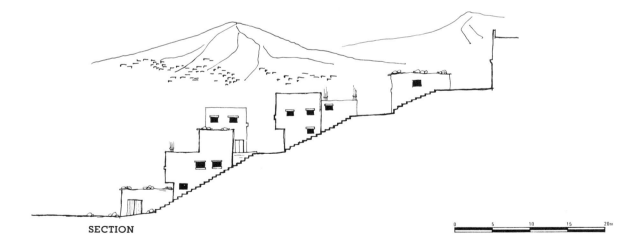

SECTION

EL AGUSTINO (Hill), Lima
DWELLING GROUP
Sources: Photographs, John F. C. Turner, 1964
Quality of information: Approximate

EL AGUSTINO (Hill), Lima Air view: street corner; group of school children watching the aircraft from which the photo was taken. Different roof types and stages of construction are shown, from mats to reinforced-concrete slabs. (*opposite page*)

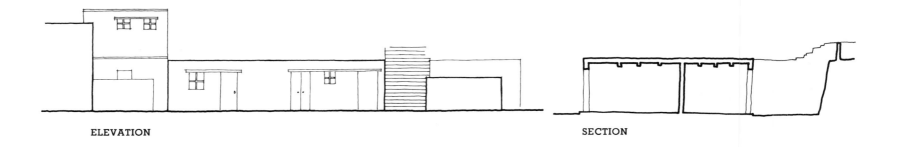

ELEVATION   SECTION

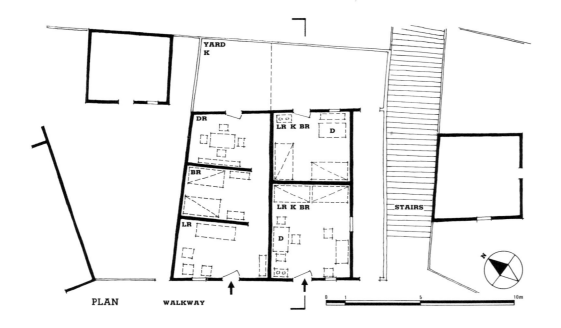

PLAN   WALKWAY

EL AGUSTINO (Hill), Lima
TYPICAL DWELLING
Sources: Photographs, John F. C. Turner, 1964
Quality of information: Approximate

DWELLING-UNIT AREAS

(large unit)	m²	%
Living (BR, DR, D, LR, K, C)	38.40	88.00
Service (T, L)	—	—
Circulation	—	—
Walls	5.00	12.00
Other	—	—
Total Unit Area:	43.40	100.00

Total Lot Area: 4.60 × 13.00 = 61.80 m², semiprivate use

LR	Living Room	**K**	Kitchen
DR	Dining Room	**L**	Laundry
D	Dining	**T**	Toilet—Bathroom
BR	Bedroom	**C**	Closet

EL AGUSTINO (Hill), Lima Group of masonry-and-concrete dwellings. Fronts of dwellings are plastered and painted. (1962) (*top left*)

Street stairs; masonry-and-concrete dwellings. Streets are active with people of all ages. (1963) (*bottom left*)

Father and daughter with rabbits. Masonry of ceramic "King Kong" bricks; reinforced-concrete lintels. (1963) (*top*)

EL AGUSTINO (Hill), Lima

Dwelling

Design and development: Squatter, progressive development.

Year of construction: 1948 (started).

Type of dwelling: Single-family row house; a group of three units are shown. "Single-family row house" in the *barriada* context means that the individually built houses abut one another; they rarely have structural, party walls.

Approximate number of people per unit: 6 people.

Approximate dwelling area per person: 7.23 sq. m (in large unit).

Layout: Two units share a common yard; one unit has no yard; there is one internal room which has no exterior openings; sometimes a small hole in the roof is provided for daylight and ventilation. While the individual dwellings on hillsides tend to be smaller than those in *barriadas* on relatively flat sites (Cuevas, El Ermitaño), room sizes are generally larger than those in the flat, higher-density localities such as El Agustino (Flat) and Mendocita.

Facilities: Cooking is performed within the house or yard; no toilet, people use garbage areas.

Components: Few small windows; exterior door openings are used to provide daylight and ventilation.

Type of construction: Masonry bearing walls of brick with reinforced-concrete slabs are used.

For comparison see the following dwellings: El Agustino (Flat), Mendocita, which are other kinds of slum dwellings; Villa Socorro, which has a similar topography.

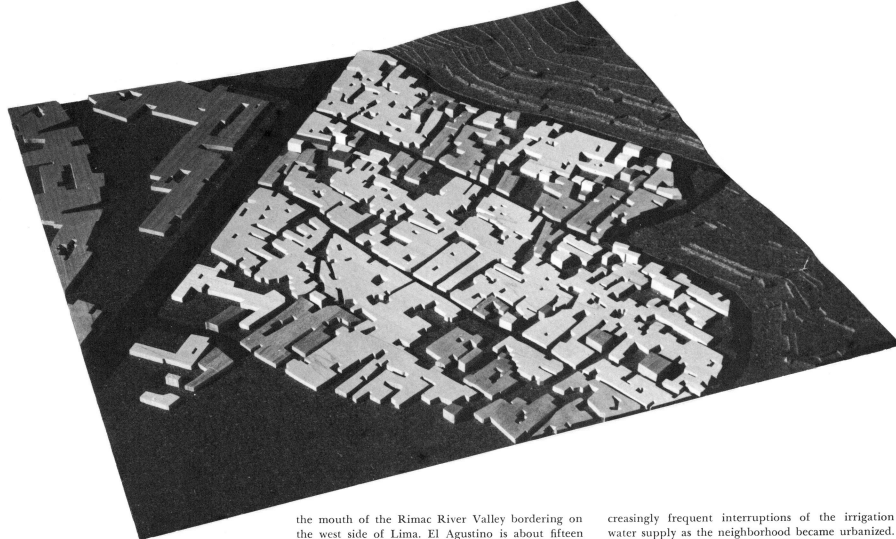

EL AGUSTINO (Flat), Lima, Peru

Location: The squatter settlement or *barriada* known as Zona 26 de El Agustino, is situated on flat, previously irrigated and intensively cultivated land. It is surrounded on three sides by the heavily built-up spurs—El Agustino (hill)—of a small mountain in the mouth of the Rimac River Valley bordering on the west side of Lima. El Agustino is about fifteen minutes' walk from the central wholesale and retail market; it is also within walking distance of the central business district and two industrial areas.

Origins: Illegal settlement by subtenants or tenant cultivators began around 1955 when the latter found subletting for residential use more profitable than market gardening. This was due partly to the increasingly frequent interruptions of the irrigation water supply as the neighborhood became urbanized. By 1960, the area was entirely occupied by dwellings, and in 1961 the locality was declared a *barrio marginal (barriada)* which absolved the occupants from the obligation to pay rents. Consequently the locality became a squatter settlement in the full sense and, officially, the land in 1965 was controlled by the government, pending its transfer to the *de facto* possessors after remodeling.

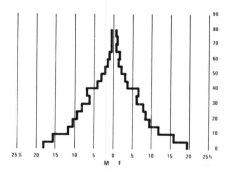

Layout: The settlement layout was determined by the footpaths and small fields between the cultivators' plots that connected a perimeter track, following an irrigation ditch at the bottom of the surrounding hillsides, and the main road, which has become an important and intensively used local thoroughfare. The individually and haphazardly determined individual plots, varying between less than fifty and several hundred square meters in area, are approached from the three principal streets via passages, most of which are blind alleys. The total area is 8.25 hectares, with a gross (1965) density of 525 persons per hectare.

Population: In 1965, there were approximately 867 households, giving an approximate total of 4,335 persons. Over 25 per cent were aggregate and extended families.

Locality Population Distribution
Survey, San Cosme, J.N.V., 1961 (equivalent)
males: M. ————; females: F. ————
horizontal: percentages; vertical: ages

EL AGUSTINO (Flat), Lima
LOCALITY PLAN
Sources: Servicio Aerofotográfico Nacional, Peru, 1961–1965
Quality of information: Approximate

EL AGUSTINO (Flat), Lima Dwellings built with adobe and straw mats; views of a pedestrian street. Trees in the background are located on the irrigated farm land.

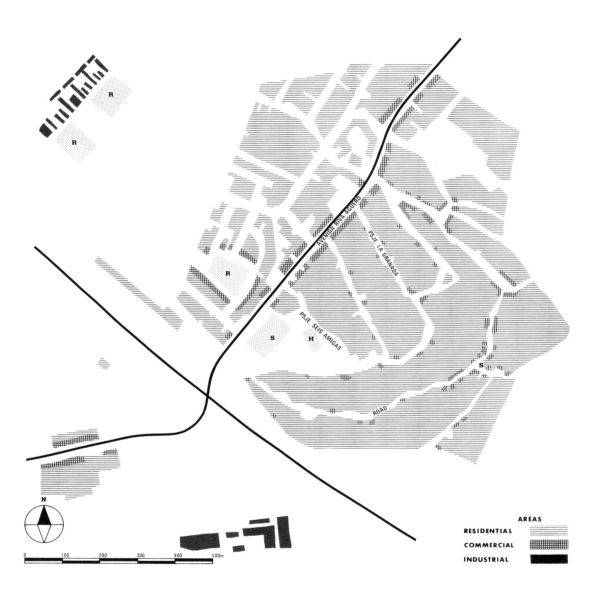

Land Use: Private dwelling lots occupy 66 per cent of the area; most of those facing the main road are used commercially and some along the internal through streets. Except for the semipublic passages and courtyards, there is practically no public space within the locality.

Incomes: Despite the physical poverty of the locality, personal incomes are relatively high; the average annual household income is U.S.$1380, 33 per cent higher than Cuevas. Unlike Mendocita, which Zone 26 resembles physically, the local population is stable and has been resident for a longer period than that of Cuevas. And Cuevas, it should be noted, has a substantially higher income level than El Ermitaño, the most recently formed *barriada*.

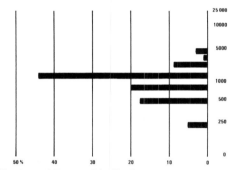

Locality Annual Income Distribution
Survey, Zona 26 (El Agustino Flat), J.C.U.S., 1965
horizontal: percentages; vertical: dollars

EL AGUSTINO (Hill, Flat), Lima
LOCALITY LAND-USE PATTERN
Sources: Servicio Aerofotográfico Nacional, Peru, 1961–1965
Quality of information: Approximate

AREAS
RESIDENTIAL
COMMERCIAL
INDUSTRIAL

H Health	Bus (solid line)	**Pk** Parking	**Ch** Church
PO Post Office	Rapid Transit	**P** Police	**R** Recreation
SS Social Services	(broken line)	**F** Fire Department	**L** Library
		S School	**U** University

EL AGUSTINO (Flat), Lima Street with El Agustino (hill) in the background. Crew digging a trench for utilities.

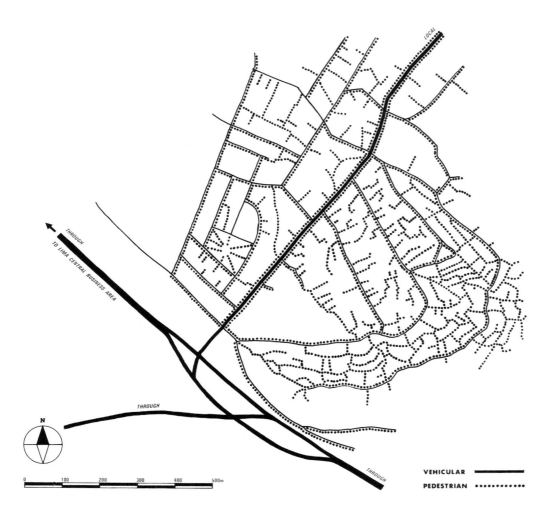

VEHICULAR ▬▬▬▬
PEDESTRIAN •••••••••

0   100   200   300   400   500m

THROUGH TO LIMA CENTRAL BUSINESS AREA

THROUGH

THROUGH

LOCAL

N

EL AGUSTINO (Flat, Hill), Lima
LOCALITY CIRCULATION PATTERN
Source: Estimate, John F. C. Turner, 1967
Quality of information: Approximate

Circulation: The through streets are generally accessible to motor vehicles but rarely used. As mentioned previously, a few passages connect these streets laterally, but the great majority are blind alleys. No roads or paths are paved. The main roads (Avenida Riva Aguero and the central highway) are served by frequent buses and many *collectivos* (collective, fixed-route taxis). The many street vendors and petty tradesmen residing in the locality use pedal tricycle carriers.

The chart illustrates the approximate availability of utilities and services at four levels: no provision at all, very limited or occasional, generally available but inadequate, and adequate or normal service.

Quality of information: Approximate

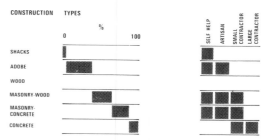

The main dwellings' construction types were grouped as follows: SHACK, ADOBE, WOOD, WOOD AND MASONRY, MASONRY AND CONCRETE, CONCRETE. The main characteristics of these types are described in the introduction.

The building industry was divided into the following groups: SELF-HELP, ARTISAN, SMALL CONTRACTOR, LARGE CONTRACTOR.

The chart shows (1) approximate percentage of each construction type within the total number of dwellings and (2) building group that generally produces each type.

Quality of information: Approximate

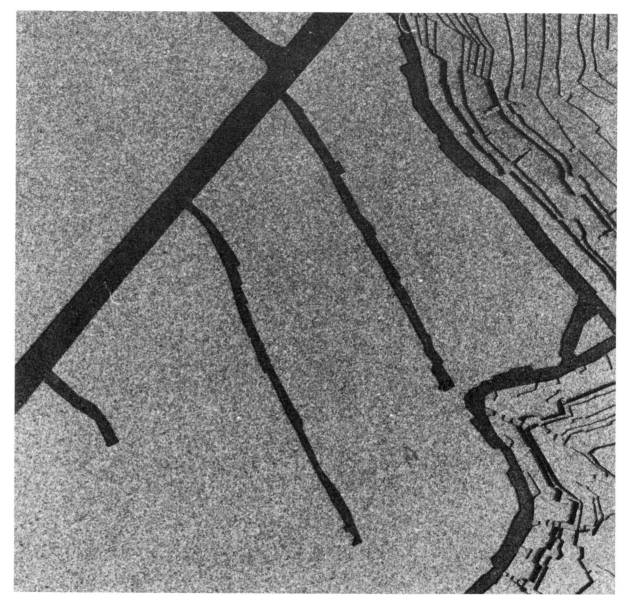

EL AGUSTINO (Flat), Lima
LOCALITY SEGMENT
400 m × 400 m; scale: 1:2500
Model of raw site showing topography, main circulation layout

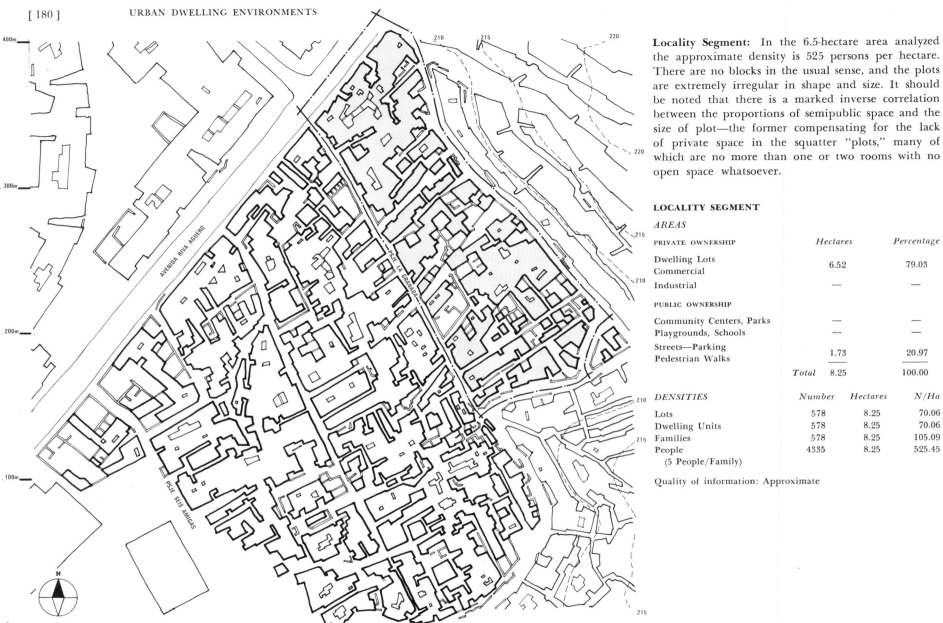

Locality Segment: In the 6.5-hectare area analyzed the approximate density is 525 persons per hectare. There are no blocks in the usual sense, and the plots are extremely irregular in shape and size. It should be noted that there is a marked inverse correlation between the proportions of semipublic space and the size of plot—the former compensating for the lack of private space in the squatter "plots," many of which are no more than one or two rooms with no open space whatsoever.

LOCALITY SEGMENT

AREAS

PRIVATE OWNERSHIP	Hectares	Percentage
Dwelling Lots	6.52	79.03
Commercial		
Industrial	—	—
PUBLIC OWNERSHIP		
Community Centers, Parks	—	—
Playgrounds, Schools	—	—
Streets—Parking	1.73	20.97
Pedestrian Walks		
Total	8.25	100.00

DENSITIES	Number	Hectares	N/Ha
Lots	578	8.25	70.06
Dwelling Units	578	8.25	70.06
Families	578	8.25	105.09
People	4335	8.25	525.45
(5 People/Family)			

Quality of information: Approximate

EL AGUSTINO (Flat), Lima
LOCALITY SEGMENT PLAN
Sources: Servicio Aerofotográfico Nacional, Peru, 1961–1965
Quality of information: Accurate

SELECTED BLOCK

AREAS

PRIVATE OWNERSHIP	Hectares	Percentage
Dwelling Lots		
Commercial	1.92	79.01
Industrial	—	—

PUBLIC OWNERSHIP		
Community Center, Parks	—	—
Playground, Schools	—	—
Streets—Parking		
Pedestrian Walks	0.57	20.99
Total	2.43	100.00

DENSITIES	Number	Hectares	N/Ha
Lots	170	2.43	69.96
Dwelling Units	170	2.43	69.96
Families	255	2.43	104.94
People	1275	2.43	524.69
(5 People/Family)			

CIRCULATION RATIO

$$\frac{\text{Circulation Length} = 1000 \text{ m}}{\text{Area} \qquad = 2.43 \text{ Ha}} = 412 \text{ m/Ha}$$

Selected block is the area enclosed by the broken line on the Locality Segment plan.

EL AGUSTINO (Flat), Lima
LOCALITY SEGMENT
400 m × 400 m; scale: 1:2500
Model of developed site showing existing buildings and streets

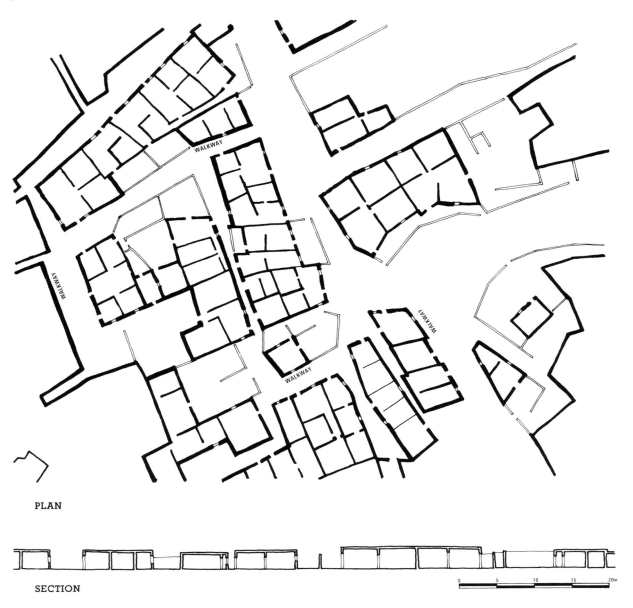

PLAN

SECTION

EL AGUSTINO (Flat), Lima
DWELLING GROUP
Sources: Photographs, John F. C. Turner, 1965
Quality of information: Approximate

Dwelling Group: The individual dwelling areas are extremely small, with an average of approximately 35 square meters. This is partly offset by the fact that half the area is open space in the form of passageways and semiprivate courtyards. Excluding the main street, three quarters of the area of Mendocita is occupied by equally small individual dwellings.

EL AGUSTINO (Flat), Lima Street; children, El Agustino (hill) in the background. A trench is still waiting for the utilities to be installed. (1965)

ELEVATION

SECTION

WALKWAY

LR K

D

K

D

LR
K

LR K BR

BR

BR

YARD

BR

K

LR

BR

BR

D

WALKWAY

PLAN

0   1   5   10m

DWELLING-UNIT AREAS

(large unit)	m^2	%
Living (BR, DR, D, LR, K, C)	18.52	51.53
Service (T, L)	—	—
Circulation	—	—
Walls	9.58	26.66
Other (yard)	7.84	21.81
Total Unit Area:	35.94	100.00

Total Lot Area: 35.94 m²

LR	Living Room	**K**	Kitchen
DR	Dining Room	**L**	Laundry
D	Dining	**T**	Toilet—Bathroom
BR	Bedroom	**C**	Closet

EL AGUSTINO (Flat), Lima
TYPICAL DWELLING
Sources: Photographs, John F. C. Turner, 1965
Quality of information: Approximate

EL AGUSTINO (Flat), Lima Street; woman with chamber pot; El Agustino (hill) in the background. (*top left*)

Court of a group of dwellings; 10 children; 5 dogs (*bottom left*)

Girl walking down a street; dogs guarding a door, "CAVE CANEM"; tree left from former farm land; El Agustino (hill) in the background (*top*)

EL AGUSTINO (Flat), Lima

Dwelling

Design and development: Squatter, progressive development.

Year of construction: 1955 (started).

Type of dwelling: Single-family houses; a group of four dwellings is shown, two of one room, two of two rooms.

Approximate number of people per unit: 6 people.

Approximate dwelling area per person: 6 sq. m (in large L unit).

Layout: Three of the units do not have a yard, leaving the narrow walkway as the only open space. One unit has a yard, partially covered where cooking is performed. Where there is no internal yard or court, ventilation and daylighting are obtained through a small opening in the roof.

Facilities: The one-room units have a kerosene stove, table, beds, and other furniture which is all crowded in a very small space. There is no toilet; people use garbage areas.

Components: Very few small windows; exterior door openings are used to provide light and ventilation.

Type of construction: With few exceptions all dwellings are of adobe bearing walls and timber on bamboo roofs covered with a thin layer of earth; a minority of dwellings have cement floors; most have mud floors.

For comparison see the following dwellings: El Agustino (Hill), Mendocita, which represent other types of *barriada* dwellings.

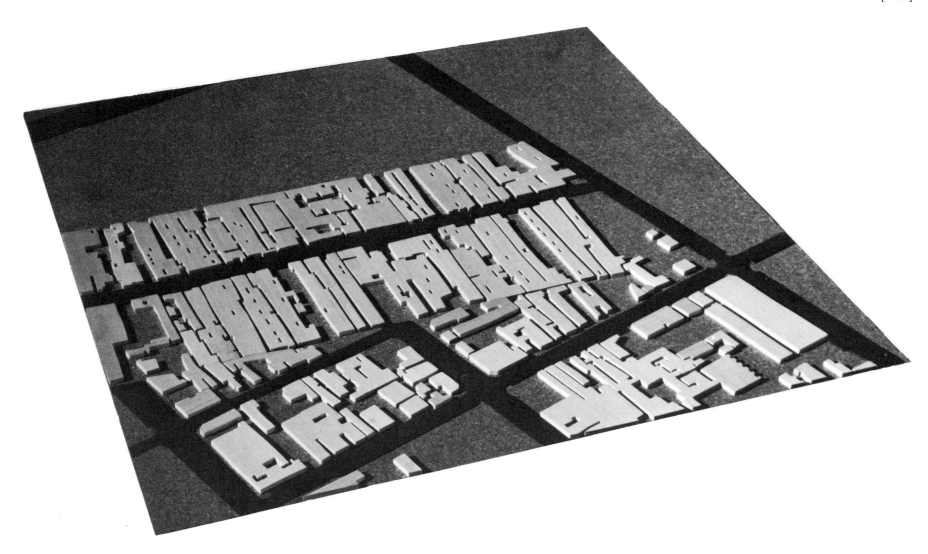

MENDOCITA, Lima, Peru

Location: Mendocita is a clandestinely built concentration of rental slum tenements originally located at the edge of the built-up area of Lima (in 1941), but well within the "Zone of Transition," or the inner ring, by 1961. Like Zone 26 of El Agustino, Mendocita was established on private, previously cultivated, flat land and is within easy walking distance of the central business district and the central markets; it is also in the heart of an area of intensive small industrial and commercial activity.

Origins: Established by the tenants or owners of the cultivated land on which it was built, and without regard for city building regulations, Mendocita was intended for renting to the lowest income sector and has maintained that function (to 1965). Government agencies have made several attempts to eradicate the locality, but vested interests proved too powerful, in spite of the damage that Mendocita's presence has caused to adjacent commercial development and land values.

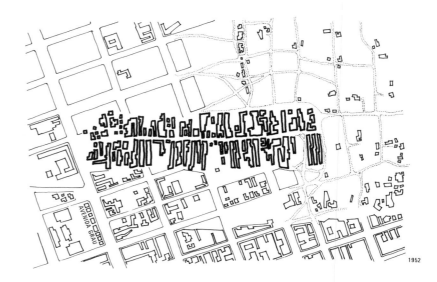

Locality Population Distribution
Caravedo *et al.*, 1956; population, 4914
males: M. ————; females: F. ————
horizontal: percentages; vertical: ages

MENDOCITA, Lima
LOCALITY PLAN Showing Three Stages of
Development
Sources: Servicio Aerofotográfico Nacional, Peru, 1942–1961
Quality of information: Approximate

Layout: Mendocita is modeled on the classic and almost universal corridor tenement. Originally, most of the passages perpendicular to the main central street also opened out to the surrounding land. After the adjacent areas had been developed, however, walls were built to contain the possible growth of Mendocita, blocking most of these openings.

Population: In 1961, the population of Mendocita was reported as 7,000, 40 per cent more than the population recorded in 1956. The age-sex pyramid shown is for 1956; it reveals a substantially higher proportion of males in the most active working-age group of twenty to forty-five years. In this respect, Mendocita is similar to Charlestown, Boston, also a low-income and relatively stagnant community. Only 10 per cent of Mendocita's adult inhabitants had lived in the locality for less than four years; the majority, 60 per cent in fact, had lived there for ten years or more. The average household was 4.7, appreciably smaller than the metropolitan and other local averages.

MENDOCITA, Lima Air view. The development has begun along a spine; farm land is all around; the urban grid is advancing (bottom of the photograph); wide street at lower left corner is still contained. (1942) (*opposite page*)

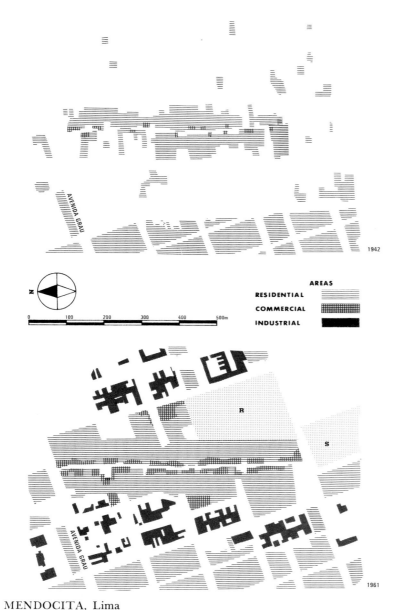

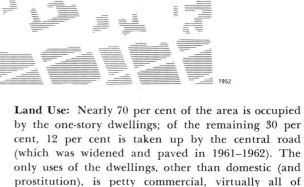

Land Use: Nearly 70 per cent of the area is occupied by the one-story dwellings; of the remaining 30 per cent, 12 per cent is taken up by the central road (which was widened and paved in 1961–1962). The only uses of the dwellings, other than domestic (and prostitution), is petty commercial, virtually all of which is concentrated along the central street.

Incomes: No statistics are available on incomes, but an analysis of occupations in 1956 shows that an exceptionally high proportion of earners are of the lowest category. Ten per cent were street vendors, and "nearly all heads of families" were classified as unskilled laborers.

MENDOCITA, Lima Air view. Ten years later. The development has changed very little, but farming is almost gone with the exception of the land shown on the right-hand side, which soon will be covered by the urban grid. The wide street has finally cut through and has been paved—Mendocita remains like a scar. (1952) (*opposite page*)

MENDOCITA, Lima
LOCALITY LAND-USE PATTERN in Three Stages
of Development
Sources: Servicio Aerofotográfico Nacional, Peru, 1941–1962
Quality of information: Approximate

H Health	Bus **(solid line)**	**Pk** Parking	**Ch** Church
PO Post Office	Rapid Transit	**P** Police	**R** Recreation
SS Social Services	**(broken line)**	**F** Fire Department	**L** Library
		S School	**U** University

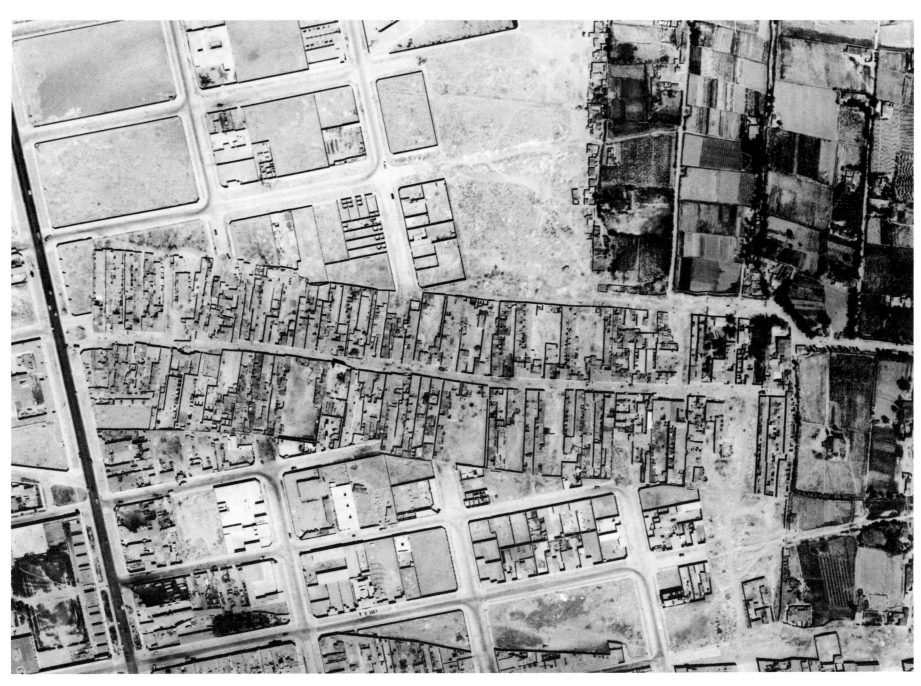

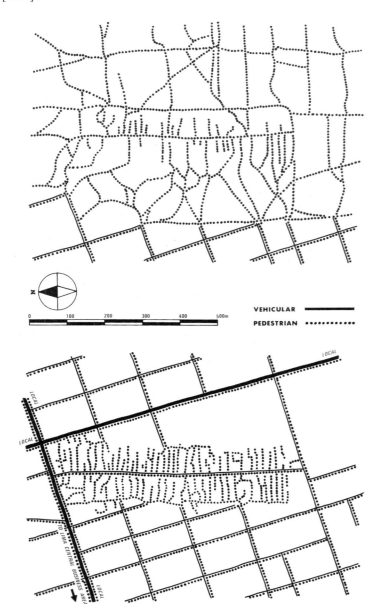

VEHICULAR ━━━━━━

PEDESTRIAN ••••••••••••

MENDOCITA, Lima
LOCALITY CIRCULATION PATTERN in Three
Stages of Development
Source: Estimate, John F. C. Turner, 1967
Quality of information: Approximate

Circulation: Initially all circulation was pedestrian; by 1955, the central street was open to vehicular traffic as a cul-de-sac, and by 1961 it was paved and connected a principal and a secondary city street. All other paths are pedestrian passages inaccessible to wheeled traffic.

UTILITIES

WATER

SEWAGE

ELECTRICITY

PAVED ROADS

TELEPHONE

SERVICES

SCHOOLS

HEALTH

REFUSE COLLECTION

PUBLIC TRANSPORT

RECREATION

FIRE

POLICE

The chart illustrates the approximate availability of utilities and services at four levels: no provision at all, very limited or occasional, generally available but inadequate, and adequate or normal service.

Quality of information: Approximate

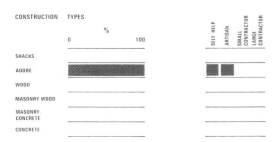

CONSTRUCTION   TYPES

%

0   100

SELF HELP
ARTISAN
SMALL CONTRACTOR
LARGE CONTRACTOR

SHACKS

ADOBE

WOOD

MASONRY-WOOD

MASONRY-CONCRETE

CONCRETE

The main dwellings' construction types were grouped as follows: SHACK, ADOBE, WOOD, WOOD AND MASONRY, MASONRY AND CONCRETE, CONCRETE. The main characteristics of these types are described in the introduction.

The building industry was divided into the following groups: SELF-HELP, ARTISAN, SMALL CONTRACTOR, LARGE CONTRACTOR.

The chart shows (1) approximate percentage of each construction type within the total number of dwellings and (2) building group that generally produces each type.

Quality of information: Approximate

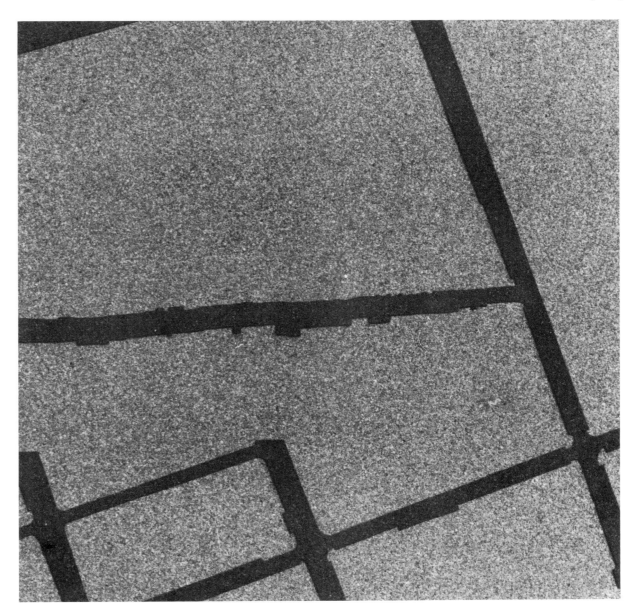

MENDOCITA, Lima
LOCALITY SEGMENT
400 m × 400 m; scale: 1:2500
Model of raw site showing topography, main circulation layout

MENDOCITA, Lima
LOCALITY SEGMENT PLAN
Sources: Servicio Aerofotográfico Nacional, Peru, 1942–1961
Quality of information: Approximate

Locality Segment: In the area analyzed (2.14 hectares) the approximate density is 555 persons per hectare on the basis of the 1956 data that the average household is 4.7 persons. But if this average had increased by 40 per cent to 6.6 persons in 1961, the density at that time would have been 777. Several of the passageways open on to internal courtyards, showing the classic tenement pattern (which was prohibited by municipal regulations in Lima in 1935). The passages are generally very narrow, between 1.2 m × 1. 5 m wide.

LOCALITY SEGMENT

AREAS

PRIVATE OWNERSHIP	Hectares	Percentage
Dwelling Lots Commercial Industrial	2.10	48.84
PUBLIC OWNERSHIP		
Community Centers, Parks	—	—
Playgrounds, Schools	—	—
Streets—Parking	0.85	19.76
Pedestrian Walks	1.35	31.40
Total	4.30	100.00

DENSITIES	Number	Hectares	N/Ha
Lots	213	4.30	49.53
Dwelling Units	213	4.30	49.53
Families	213	4.30	49.53
People	1065	4.30	247.67
(5 People/Family)			

Quality of information: Approximate

SELECTED BLOCK

AREAS

PRIVATE OWNERSHIP	*Hectares*	*Percentage*
Dwelling Lots Commercial	1.49	69.63
Industrial	—	—
PUBLIC OWNERSHIP		
Community Center, Parks	—	—
Playground, Schools	—	—
Streets—Parking Pedestrian Walks	0.65	30.37
Total	2.14	100.00

DENSITIES	*Number*	*Hectares*	*N/Ha*
Lots	71	2.14	33.18
Dwelling Units	71	2.14	33.18
Families	71	2.14	33.18
People (5 People/Family)	355	2.14	165.89

CIRCULATION RATIO

$$\frac{\text{Circulation Length} = 1795 \text{ m}}{\text{Area} \quad = 2.14 \text{ Ha}} = 839 \text{ m/Ha}$$

Selected block is the area enclosed by the broken line on the Locality Segment plan.

MENDOCITA, Lima
LOCALITY SEGMENT
400 m × 400 m; scale: 1:2500
Model of developed site showing existing buildings and streets

Dwelling Groups: If all the dwellings shown in the plan of the dwelling group were occupied by average-size households, the density would be over 1,200 persons per hectare, and the capacity of the locality would be approximately 11,000 persons. The public or semiprivate passageways and courts compensating for the lack of enclosed dwelling space is less than half that provided in El Agustino (flat) or about 14 per cent, taking into account a 2-meter strip of the central street.

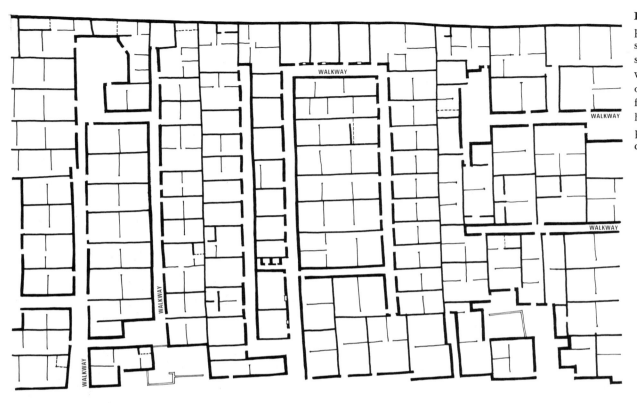

WALKWAY

STREET

PLAN

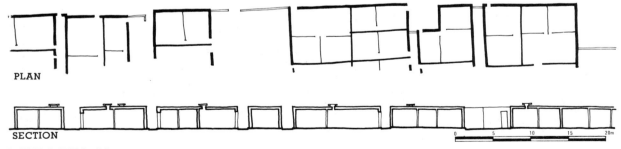

SECTION

MENDOCITA, Lima
DWELLING GROUP
Sources: Servicio Aerofotográfico Nacional, Peru, 1961; photographs, John F. C. Turner, 1963
Quality of information: Approximate

MENDOCITA, Lima A dramatic view of the clash between Mendocita and the urban grid. Bus, truck, and auto repair shops. (1961)

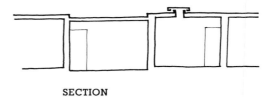

ELEVATION

SECTION

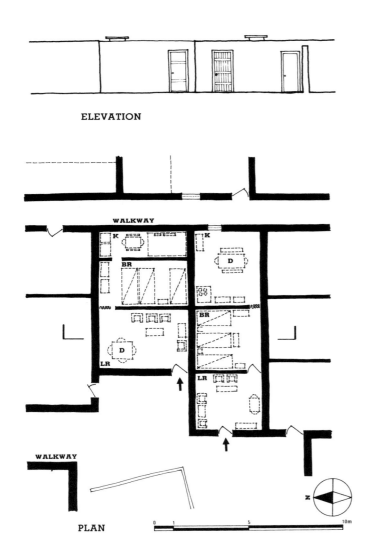

PLAN

MENDOCITA, Lima
TYPICAL DWELLING
Sources: Servicio Aerofotográfico Nacional, Peru, 1941–1962
Quality of information: Approximate

DWELLING-UNIT AREAS

(long unit)	m^2	%
Living (BR, DR, D, LR, K, C)	36.70	80.90
Service (T, L)	—	—
Circulation	—	—
Walls	8.90	19.10
Other	—	—
Total Unit Area:	45.60	100.00

Total Lot Area: 4.00 × 11.40 = 45.60 m²

LR	Living Room	**K**	Kitchen
DR	Dining Room	**L**	Laundry
D	Dining	**T**	Toilet—Bathroom
BR	Bedroom	**C**	Closet

LIMA A typical alley in a slum similar to Mendocita: people, a cart, a car, an open shop, a peddler. (*opposite page*)

MENDOCITA, Lima

Dwelling

Design and development: Clandestine slum development.

Year of construction: 1938 (started).

Type of dwelling: Three-room row dwellings (also one- and two-room units not shown here) are typical of the poorer type of slum housing.

Approximate number of people per unit: 8 people.

Approximate dwelling area per person: 5.70 sq. m (in long unit).

Layout: The interior room of the three-room unit has no daylight or ventilation. Sometimes when there is no internal yard or court, ventilation and daylighting are obtained through a small opening in the roof. Almost all the area of the small rooms is occupied with beds. There are no yards; the only open space available is public or semipublic courts and alleys.

Facilities: A stove and a table are in the back room; the stove is usually a charcoal or a "Primus" (a kerosene pressure) type. There is no toilet; people use garbage areas.

Components: Exterior door openings are used to provide light and ventilation.

Type of construction: Adobe bearing walls; mat roof with mud covering; earth floor.

For comparison see the following dwellings: El Agustino (Hill, flat), which are also slum dwellings.

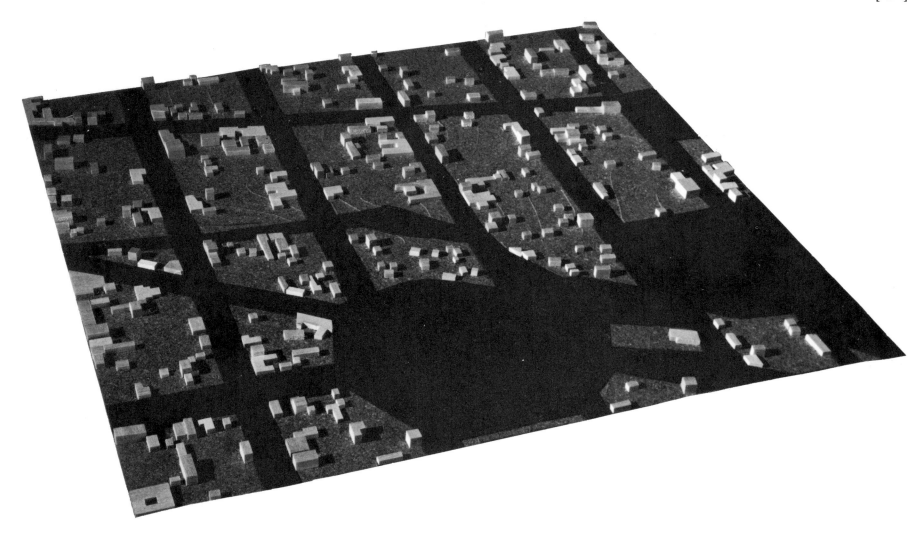

MARIANO MELGAR, Arequipa, Peru

Location: Mariano Melgar, a squatter settlement, known locally as an *Urbanización Popular,* is situated to the southeast of the city of Arequipa, on the lowest slopes formed by lava flows from the now-extinct volcano Misti. It is half an hour's walk from the center of the city and is diametrically opposite the industrial zone to which the locality connects by bus routes.

Origins: The locality was settled around 1950, probably by an organized group of citizens. In 1957, about 50 per cent of the plots were still vacant, but almost all were occupied by buildings under construction by 1965. Claimed by the local suburban municipality of Miraflores as being under its jurisdiction from the beginning, it had in fact been incorporated into that municipality by 1965.

MARIANO MELGAR, Arequipa
LOCALITY PLAN
Sources: Census Map O.A.T.A., Arequipa, 1957
Quality of information: Accurate

Layout: The plan of Mariano Melgar is an extension of the grid-iron street system of the adjacent suburb of Miraflores. In general the land surface is on an even gradient, but there is one dry gulley formed by very occasional storm water. The total area of approximately 50 hectares would have had a population of approximately 3,000 persons in 1956, rising to approximately 7,000 in 1965; the density in the later year would have been, therefore, approximately 85 persons per hectare.

Population: No data is available on the age-sex composition of Mariano Melgar. The data for a neighboring area in 1963, however, is likely to have been similar for the former in 1956–1957. The average age (for the *barriada* Manuel Prado in 1963) was about fourteen years; 90 per cent of the population was divided into two groups, equally balanced between the sexes. The 60 per cent under twenty years has an average age of eight years, and the 30 per cent between twenty-five and forty-five years has an average age of thirty-three years. As is usual with newly settled peri-urban settlements, the population was composed very largely of young nuclear families.

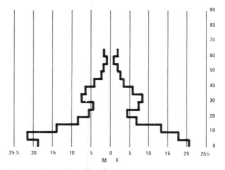

Locality Population Distribution
Survey, Manuel Prado, J.N.V., 1965 (equivalent)
males: M. ————; females: F. ————
horizontal: percentages; vertical: dollars

MARIANO MELGAR, Arequipa Air view. The large rectangular space is a soccer field. The equally large but round space is of unknown use. Streets are barren, but trees grow in the backyards of the lots. (1965) (*opposite page*)

Land Use: Approximately 70 per cent of the area is occupied by private dwelling lots, a small number of which are used for petty commerce and artisan workshops; these are scattered quite evenly over the settlement. About 6 per cent of the area has been set aside for recreational use—in the aerial photograph it can be seen that the rectangular plaza is used as a football pitch. The information available reveals only one school within the settlement, but there are others in the immediate vicinity.

Incomes: Continuing with the assumption that the data for Manuel Prado for 1963 are comparable with the data for Mariano Melgar in 1956–1957, the average annual household income would have been U.S. $612. This is almost exactly the same as the average personal-income level in the city Arequipa as a whole in 1964.

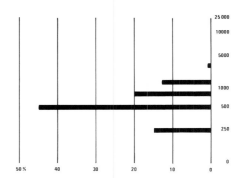

Locality Annual Income Distribution
Survey, Manuel Prado, 1963, J.N.V.
households, 325 (equivalent)
horizontal: percentages; vertical: dollars

MARIANO MELGAR, Arequipa
LOCALITY LAND-USE PATTERN
Sources: Census Map, O.A.T.A., Arequipa, 1957
Quality of information: Approximate

H Health	Bus **(solid line)**	**Pk** Parking	**Ch** Church
PO Post Office	Rapid Transit	**P** Police	**R** Recreation
SS Social Services	**(broken line)**	**F** Fire Department	**L** Library
		S School	**U** University

AREAS

RESIDENTIAL

COMMERCIAL

INDUSTRIAL

0   100   200   300   400   500m

Arequipa Air view (1957) of a clandestine subdivision, similar to Mariano Melgar, established in 1932. (Blocks approximately 100 × 100 m.) Streets are wide; lots and dwellings are fairly large. Dwelling in different stages of construction are shown. All the properties are fenced with a masonry wall.

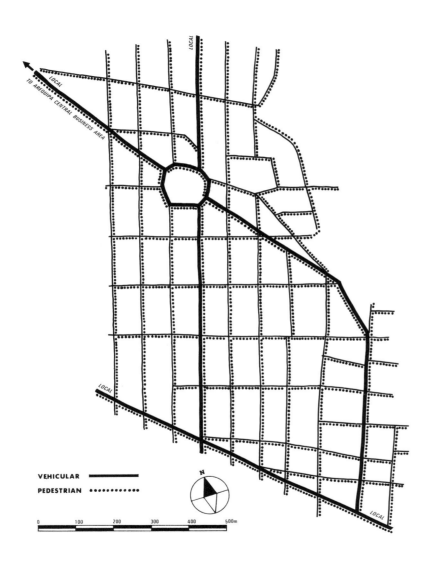

VEHICULAR ━━━━━
PEDESTRIAN ••••••••••

0   100   200   300   400   500m

MARIANO MELGAR, Arequipa
LOCALITY CIRCULATION PATTERN
Source: Estimate, John F. C. Turner, 1967
Quality of information: Tentative

Circulation: Except for urban streets interrupted by dry gulleys, large rocks, and patches of deep, loose sand, all streets are accessible to vehicular traffic. There are two regular bus routes passing through the locality, connecting it with the neighboring squatter areas and the city.

The chart illustrates the approximate availability of utilities and services at four levels: no provision at all, very limited or occasional, generally available but inadequate, and adequate or normal service.

Quality of information: Approximate

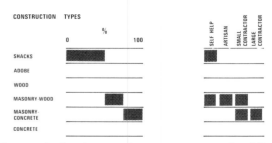

The main dwellings' construction types were grouped as follows: SHACK, ADOBE, WOOD, WOOD AND MASONRY, MASONRY AND CONCRETE, CONCRETE. The main characteristics of these types are described in the introduction.

The building industry was divided into the following groups: SELF-HELP, ARTISAN, SMALL CONTRACTOR, LARGE CONTRACTOR.

The chart shows (1) approximate percentage of each construction type within the total number of dwellings and (2) building group that generally produces each type.

Quality of information: Approximate

MARIANO MELGAR, Arequipa
LOCALITY SEGMENT
400 m × 400 m; scale: 1:2500
Model of raw site showing topography, main circulation layout

Locality Segment: In the 9.7-hectare area analyzed, 61 per cent of the area is occupied by private lots. Typically the blocks are approximately 120 m × 60 m. Streets vary in width, the majority being 12 m and 18 m wide.

LOCALITY SEGMENT

AREAS

PRIVATE OWNERSHIP	Hectares	Percentage
Dwelling Lots	9.72	60.75
Commercial		
Industrial	—	—
PUBLIC OWNERSHIP		
Community Centers, Parks	—	—
Playgrounds, Schools	—	—
Streets—Parking	6.28	39.25
Pedestrian Walks		
Total	16.00	100.00

DENSITIES	Number	Hectares	N/Ha
Lots	216	16.00	13.50
Dwelling Units	216	16.00	13.50
Families	183	16.00	11.44
People	1006	16.00	62.88
(5.5 People/Family)			

Quality of information: Approximate

MARIANO MELGAR, Arequipa
LOCALITY SEGMENT PLAN
Sources: Census Map, O.A.T.A., Arequipa, 1957
Quality of information: Accurate

SELECTED BLOCK

AREAS

PRIVATE OWNERSHIP	*Hectares*	*Percentage*
Dwelling Lots Commercial	0.74	69.16
Industrial	—	—
PUBLIC OWNERSHIP		
Community Center, Parks	—	—
Playground, Schools	—	—
Streets—Parking Pedestrian Walks	0.33	30.84
Total	1.07	100.00

DENSITIES	*Number*	*Hectares*	*N/Ha*
Lots	21	1.07	19.63
Dwelling Units	17	1.07	15.89
Families	17	1.07	15.89
People	93	1.07	86.91
(5.5 People/Family)			

CIRCULATION RATIO

$$\frac{\text{Circulation Length} = 220 \text{ m}}{\text{Area} \qquad = 1.07 \text{ Ha}} = 206 \text{ m/Ha}$$

Selected block is the area enclosed by the broken line on the Locality Segment plan.

MARIANO MELGAR, Arequipa
LOCALITY SEGMENT
400 m × 400 m; scale: 1:2500
Model of developed site showing existing buildings and streets

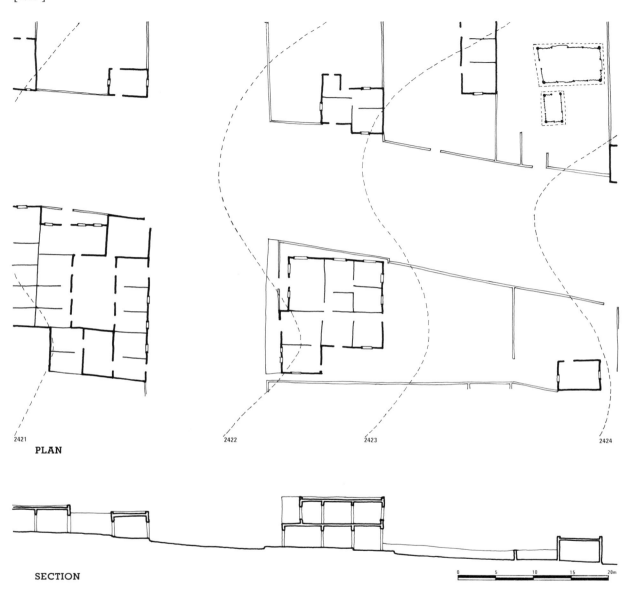

Dwelling Group: The majority of the plots have an area of 320 square meters (12 m × 30 m). The most common house plans are the traditional courtyard model and the outward looking modern "chalet" type. All dwellings are individually designed and built according to widely differing schedules. Few dwellings were complete, even by 1965, 15 years after settlement and development started.

2421

PLAN

2422   2423   2424

SECTION

0   5   10   15   20m

MARIANO MELGAR, Arequipa
DWELLING GROUP
Sources: Photographs, John F. C. Turner, 1965
Quality of information: Approximate

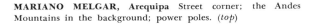

MARIANO MELGAR, Arequipa Street corner; the Andes Mountains in the background; power poles. (*top*)

The wide dirt streets; a bus; dwellings in permanent construction. (*top right*)

Children at a public well; tin and ceramic containers. Compare with street well at El Gallo. (*bottom right*)

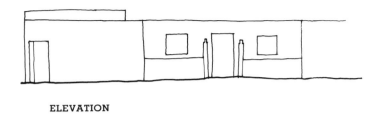

ELEVATION

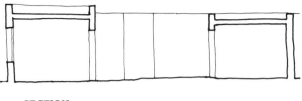

SECTION

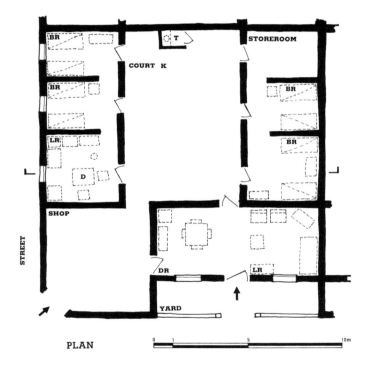

PLAN

0   1   5   10m

MARIANO MELGAR, Arequipa
TYPICAL DWELLING
Sources: Photographs, John F. C. Turner, 1965
Quality of information: Approximate

DWELLING-UNIT AREAS

	m^2	%
Living (BR, DR, D, LR, K, C)	141.69	63.98
Service (T, L)	0.96	0.43
Circulation	—	—
Walls	40.09	18.10
Other (shop, storeroom)	38.74	17.49
Total Unit Area:	221.48	100.00

Total Lot Area: 15.00 × 16.00 = 240.00 m², semiprivate use

LR	Living Room	**K**	Kitchen
DR	Dining Room	**L**	Laundry
D	Dining	**T**	Toilet—Bathroom
BR	Bedroom	**C**	Closet

MARIANO MELGAR, Arequipa Construction crew pouring a reinforced-concrete slab. Notice the number of people that participate in the operation. See construction in El Gallo. (*top*)

Dwellings; the snow-capped Andes in the background. (1957) (*top right*)

Lima Squatters huts. Low stone walls provide some protection against wind; roofs are of canvas and mats. (*bottom right*)

MARIANO MELGAR, Arequipa

Dwelling

Design and development: Squatter, progressive development.

Year of construction: 1950 (started).

Type of dwelling: Multifamily row house with shop, corner lot. "Single-family row house" in the *barriada* context means that the individually built houses abut one another; they rarely have structural, party walls.

Approximate number of people per unit: 10 people.

Approximate dwelling area per person: 18.26 sq. m.

Layout: The dwelling shown is of the traditional courtyard type, rarely found in Lima. It is on a subdivided lot of 249 sq. m, considerably larger than the average in Lima but smaller than the average in the locality. Two related families share the dwelling.

Facilities: Cooking is done in the courtyard; the courtyard also contains a latrine.

Components: Exterior door openings are used to provide light and ventilation; rooms are connected internally by openings without doors.

Type of construction: Masonry bearing walls built from sillar, a white pumice or volcanic rock, with reinforced-concrete piers in the corners with a poured-concrete roof; the floors would be of cement, with wood parquet in the main living or reception room; internal walls and ceilings would be plastered.

For comparison see the following dwellings: Cuevas, El Ermitaño, which are also designed by squatters.

EL GALLO, Ciudad Guayana, Venezuela

Location: El Gallo is a development sponsored by the Corporación Venezolana de Guayana (C.V.G.) as part of the Ciudad Guayana Development Program. Urban District 112 (El Gallo) is located 1.5 kilometers east of the center of the old town of San Felix on property of the C.V.G. The land surface slopes evenly toward the Orinoco River; the laterite soil, with a natural cover of grass and shrubs, can be easily eroded during the rainy season if precautions are not taken when developing the land.

Origins: Urban District 112 was settled in 1964, the first of a series of similar "progressive development" areas for low-income families, designed to satisfy the demand hitherto resulting in widespread squatting. The progressive development principle is based on the priority of secure land tenure and essential community facilities—building lots, graded-but-unsurfaced streets, schools, and so forth, being provided before dwelling unit and public utilities. The latter are built in stages after the owner-occupiers establish themselves in provisional shacks. By 1967, almost all the plots had completed dwellings.

Layout: The locality was planned with a large central area reserved for school, playgrounds, community services, and commercial facilities. The layout makes an awkward use of the topography and has aggravated erosion problems.

Population: In 1963–1964, El Gallo had a population of approximately 300 families. In 1967, a sample of thirty families revealed a somewhat asymmetrical age-sex distribution over the average age of fifteen years. There were many more male than female adolescents, probably because the girls are employed as resident servants. The great majority of the adults (72 per cent) are under forty-five, the average age of the adult women being twenty-nine and that of the adult men thirty-one.

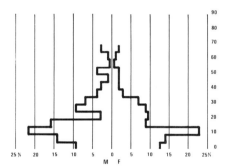

Locality Population Distribution
C.S.E.D. Census, 1967; UD-112 (sample 30 families)
males: M. ———; females: F. ———
horizontal: percentages; vertical: ages

EL GALLO, Ciudad Guayana
LOCALITY PLAN
Sources: Maps, Corporación Venezolana de Guayana, 1963–1965
Quality of information: Accurate

EL GALLO, Ciudad Guayana Man-made erosion: the site was bulldozed and the protective ground cover removed; the natural drainage was destroyed but not replaced, and when the cycle of heavy rains came, the water ran down removing the earth around hill dwellings, leaving foundations exposed, and covering the floors of dwellings below with a thick layer of mud. The Orinoco River in the background. (1967)

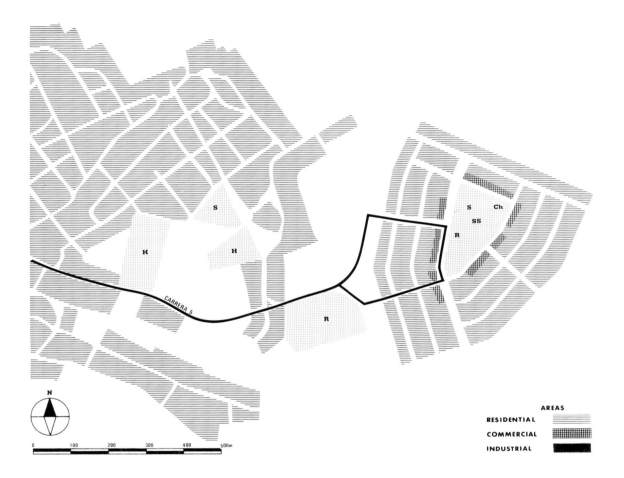

N

| 0 | 100 | 200 | 300 | 400 | 500m |

AREAS

RESIDENTIAL

COMMERCIAL

INDUSTRIAL

Land Use: Privately owned dwellings occupy approximately 42 per cent of the developed area; approximately 30 per cent is reserved for public use and the remaining 28 per cent for streets. As noted, the plan anticipates the concentration of community services in the interior open area where the institutional facilities have been installed; field observation has revealed that the local shops are scattered throughout the area as in the other low-income localities surveyed.

Incomes: The average annual household income in the locality, from the 1967 sample survey, was U.S. $766, approximately 60 per cent of the average for the city as a whole.

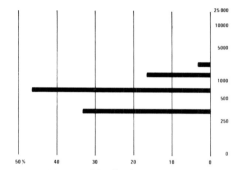

Locality Annual Income Distribution
Survey, 1965, UD-112
horizontal: percentages; vertical: dollars

EL GALLO, Ciudad Guayana
LOCALITY LAND-USE PATTERN
Sources: Maps, Corporación Venezolana de Guayana, 1963–1965
Quality of information: Approximate

H	Health	Bus (**solid line**)
PO	Post Office	Rapid Transit
SS	Social Services	(**broken line**)

Pk	Parking	**Ch**	Church
P	Police	**R**	Recreation
F	Fire Department	**L**	Library
S	School	**U**	University

EL GALLO, Ciudad Guayana Street; the Orinoco River in the background, a public fountain in the foreground. Dwellings that do not have water take turns in connecting a hose to the faucets. Compare with the public fountain at Mariano Melgar, Arequipa, Peru, where the water is carried to the dwellings in containers. (1967)

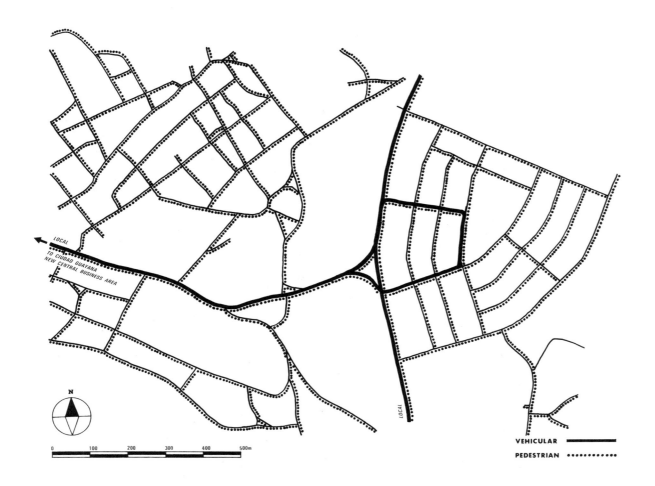

VEHICULAR ━━━━━━

PEDESTRIAN •••••••••••

EL GALLO, Ciudad Guayana
LOCALITY CIRCULATION PATTERN
Source: Estimate, Horacio Caminos, 1967
Quality of information: Approximate

Circulation: All streets are accessible to both pedestrian and vehicular traffic, but there are a series of connecting open spaces that can be crossed on foot but not by wheeled traffic. Two avenues, 25.20 meters wide, lead nowhere. A regular bus service makes a detour into the locality with a stop at the central area.

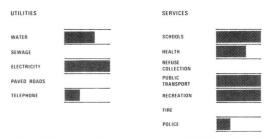

The chart illustrates the approximate availability of utilities and services at four levels: no provision at all, very limited or occasional, generally available but inadequate, and adequate or normal service.

Quality of information: Approximate

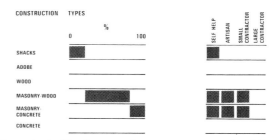

The main dwellings' construction types were grouped as follows: SHACK, ADOBE, WOOD, WOOD AND MASONRY, MASONRY AND CONCRETE, CONCRETE. The main characteristics of these types are described in the introduction.

The building industry was divided into the following groups: SELF-HELP, ARTISAN, SMALL CONTRACTOR, LARGE CONTRACTOR.

The chart shows (1) approximate percentage of each construction type within the total number of dwellings and (2) building group that generally produces each type.

Quality of information: Approximate

EL GALLO, Ciudad Guayana
LOCALITY SEGMENT
400 m × 400 m; scale: 1:2500
Model of raw site showing topography, main circulation layout

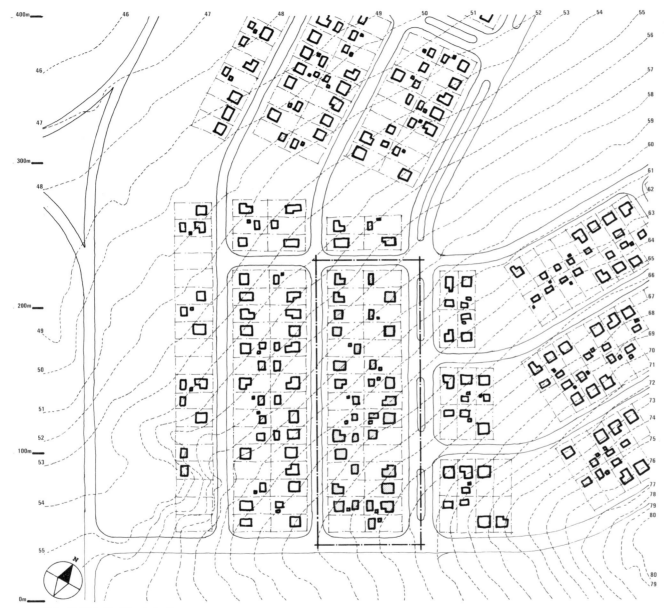

Locality Segment: All privately owned land is divided into regular dwelling plots of 300 square meters (12 m × 25 m); some blocks are only one plot deep (25 m), and the lengths vary between 24 m (2 plots wide) and well over 200 m. Where changes of direction occur in the blocks, breaks have been made creating wedge-shaped open spaces of indeterminate use.

LOCALITY SEGMENT

AREAS

PRIVATE OWNERSHIP	Hectares	Percentage
Dwelling Lots Commercial	5.44	48.57
Industrial	—	—
PUBLIC OWNERSHIP		
Community Centers, Parks Playgrounds, Schools	2.32	20.72
Streets—Parking Pedestrian Walks	3.44	30.71
Total	11.20	100.00

DENSITIES	Number	Hectares	N/Ha
Lots	189	16.00	11.81
Dwelling Units	169	16.00	10.56
Families	169	16.00	10.56
People	1014	16.00	63.38
(6.0 People/Family)			

Quality of information: Approximate

EL GALLO, Ciudad Guayana
LOCALITY SEGMENT PLAN
Sources: Maps, Corporación Venezolana de Guayana; Aerial
    Photograph, 1967
Quality of information: Approximate

SELECTED BLOCK

AREAS

PRIVATE OWNERSHIP		Hectares	Percentage
Dwelling Lots		0.87	66.41
Commercial			
Industrial		—	—
PUBLIC OWNERSHIP			
Community Center, Parks		—	—
Playground, Schools		—	—
Streets—Parking		0.44	33.59
Pedestrian Walks			
	Total	1.31	100.00

DENSITIES	Number	Hectares	N/Ha
Lots	30	1.31	22.90
Dwelling Units	27	1.31	20.61
Families	27	1.31	20.61
People	162	1.31	123.66
(6.0 People/Family)			

CIRCULATION RATIO

$$\frac{\text{Circulation Length} = 262 \text{ m}}{\text{Area} \qquad = 1.31 \text{ Ha}} = 200 \text{ m/Ha}$$

Selected block is the area enclosed by the broken line on the Locality Segment plan.

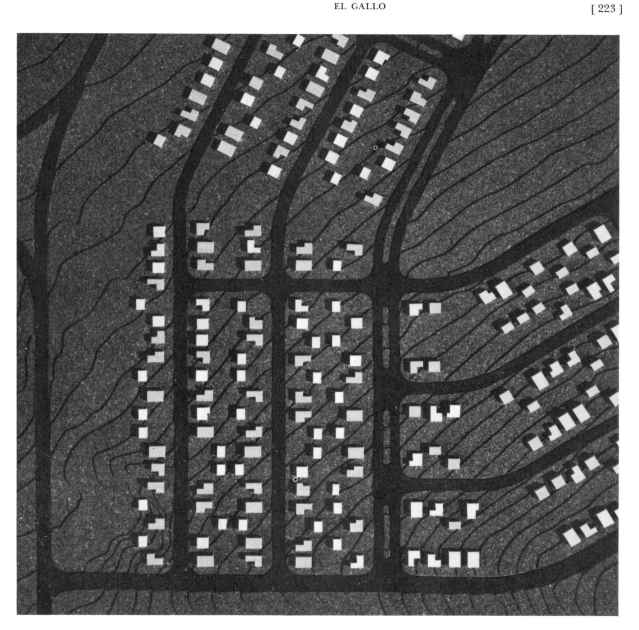

EL GALLO, Ciudad Guayana
LOCALITY SEGMENT
400 m × 400 m; scale: 1:2500
Model of developed site showing existing buildings and streets

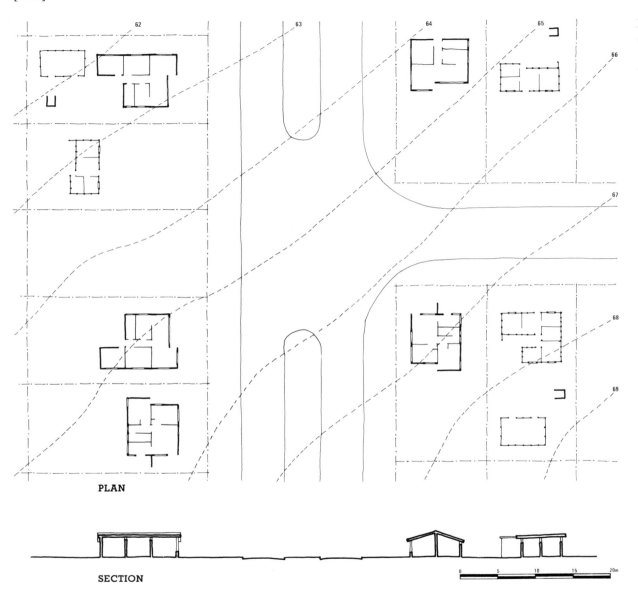

PLAN

SECTION

Dwelling Groups: There are two common types of dwellings: a standard "rural" type, built under a national government rural-housing program, and a specially designed unit for self-help construction for which loans are made to cover materials, specialized labor, and technical assistance. As residents are obliged to accept one or the other, or to build to similar standards on their own account, the great majority of the plots are built-up.

EL GALLO, Ciudad Guayana
DWELLING GROUP
Sources: Drawings, Corporación Venezolana de Guayana, 1963–
        1965
Quality of information: Approximate

EL GALLO, Ciudad Guayana Dwellings, early stage of a corner shop. (1967) *(top)*

Dwellings. The sign reads, "BARBER SHOP, OPEN SATURDAYS AND SUNDAYS," which indicates that the owner has a regular primary employment and supplements his income in his free time. (1967) *(top right)*

Shopkeeper; empty soft-drink bottles; a kerosene lamp to light the shop. (1967) *(bottom right)*

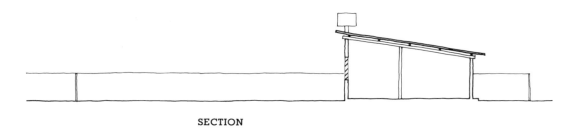

SECTION

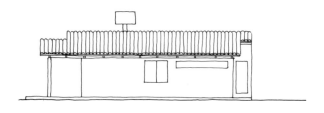

ELEVATION

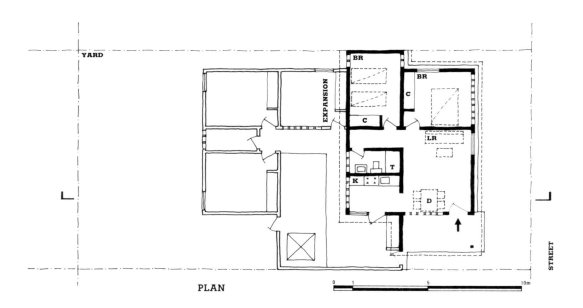

PLAN

EL GALLO, Ciudad Guayana
TYPICAL DWELLING
Sources: Drawings, Corporación Venezolana de Guayana, 1963–
1965
Qualtiy of information: Accurate

DWELLING-UNIT AREAS

	m^2	%
Living (BR, DR, D, LR, K, C)	41.86	64.39
Service (T, L)	3.24	4.98
Circulation	2.80	4.32
Walls	9.50	14.62
Other (porch)	7.60	11.69
Total Unit Area:	65.00	100.00

Total Lot Area: $12.00 \times 25.00 = 300.00$ m², private use

LR	Living Room	**K**	Kitchen
DR	Dining Room	**L**	Laundry
D	Dining	**T**	Toilet—Bathroom
BR	Bedroom	**C**	Closet

EL GALLO, Ciudad Guayana Street, masonry-and-aluminum dwellings; man-made erosion. (1967) (*bottom right*)

Dwelling construction: wood frame, aluminum roofs. Compare with construction of a dwelling in Mariano Melgar, Arequipa, Peru. (1967) (*top right*)

Street, dwellings, utility trench. (1967) (*top*)

EL GALLO, Ciudad Guayana

Dwelling

Design and development: Government autonomous agency, progressive development.

Year of construction: 1963 (started).

Type of dwelling: Single-family detached house.

Approximate number of people per unit: 6 people.

Approximate dwelling area per person: 10.83 sq. m.

Layout: The dwelling has a front and a back entrance; a small corridor is provided for future expansion. All the lots of this subdivision are equal and of 12 m × 25 m or 300 sq. m. The width of 12 m is extremely large for the nature of the subdivision; yet the dwellings promoted by the developers are not suited for the lots because they leave narrow and useless side yards.

Facilities: Back-to-back kitchen-toilet plumbing.

Components: Like Villa Socorro, perforated walls are used instead of windows to provide ventilation, security, and some light. But in El Gallo water pours into the dwelling through the perforated wall because no adequate protection has been provided against rain and wind.

Type of construction: Masonry bearing walls of 20 × 20 × 40 centimeters concrete blocks; roof of corrugated metal on wood beams.

For comparison see the following dwellings: Villa Socorro, which is also designed by "experts"; Cuevas, Mariano Melgar, which are designed by squatters with no professional help.

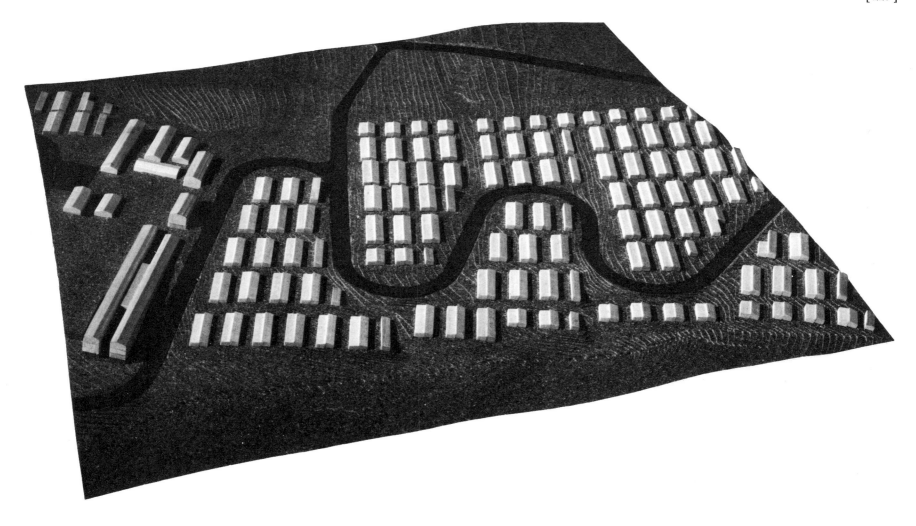

VILLA SOCORRO, Medellín, Colombia

Location: Villa Socorro is a privately developed, low-cost housing development situated on a steep hillside about 6 kilometers from the central business district of Medellín. It is surrounded on two sides by low-income residential areas. There are several important industries nearby, some within a walking distance of fifteen minutes, although the main industrial district of Medellín is on the other extreme of the valley.

Origin: Villa Socorro was developed by Casitas de la Providencia, a nonprofit foundation created in 1956 to build dwellings for low-income families. The aim of the Foundation was to help with the relocation of extremely poor families that live in slums and squatter settlements. The foundation has developed few small neighborhoods. Villa Socorro was started in 1961. Today it is completed and has been expanded uphill.

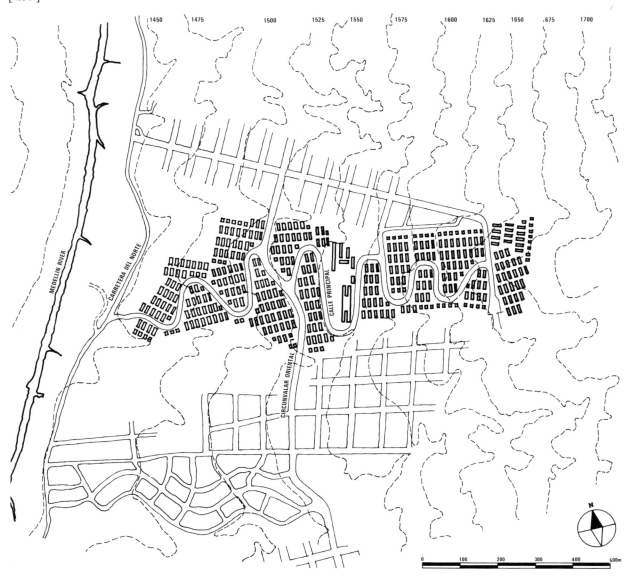

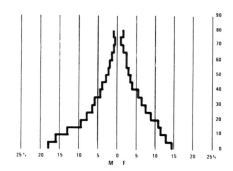

Layout: The subdivision system is determined by the topography, which is very steep (25 per cent slope). A main vehicular road winds from the bottom to the top of the locality following a 10 per cent maximum slope. Pedestrian sidewalks, running perpendicular to the contours, serving the lots. (The straight street shown on the map, running perpendicularly to the contours, is accessible only by pedestrians because it is too steep for vehicular use.)

Population: The population of Villa Socorro was 7,021 inhabitants in 1966. Of this total 22 per cent were under seven years old; 50 per cent were between eight and fifteen years old. There were about 1,030 at an average of 6.8 people per dwelling.

Locality Population Distribution
Census, 1964, Medellín
population, 772,900 (equivalent)
males: M. ————; females: F. ————
horizontal: percentages; vertical: ages

VILLA SOCORRO, Medellín
LOCALITY PLAN
Sources: Fundación Casitas de la Providencia, Medellín, 1964
Quality of information: Accurate

VILLA SOCORRO, Medellín View showing Villa Socorro and surroundings. Two ravines that bound the locality can be seen to the right and left. The valley's foothills are gradually being covered by squatters and new developments. (1968)

Land Use: Privately owned dwelling plots occupy approximately 37 per cent of the built-up area, a small proportion of which are used for minor commercial enterprises; these are not concentrated but distributed mainly along the vehicular road. A community center (school, church, social services, small soccer field) is located at a medium altitude and within maximum distances of 500 meters from the farthest dwellings. This is a reasonable walking distance in a flat or gentle terrain. But in the present case, because of the great slope, the distance becomes too painful to cover. In sloped terrains, horizontal circulation is obviously the easiest (donkey paths); in consequence, areas served from a point are not circles but rather ellipses with a major axis parallel to the contours.

Incomes: In 1966, no households were recorded as having incomes above U.S.$1,330 per annum; 92.5 per cent were reported with annual incomes below U.S.$864.

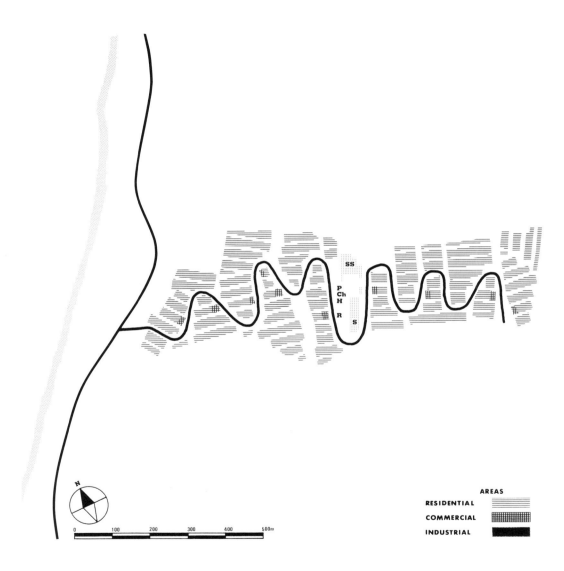

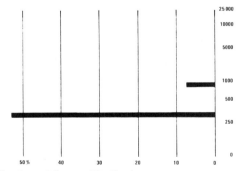

Locality Annual Income Distribution
Survey, 1966; population, 7,021
horizontal: percentages; vertical: dollars

AREAS

RESIDENTIAL

COMMERCIAL

INDUSTRIAL

VILLA SOCORRO, Medellín
LOCALITY LAND-USE PATTERN
Sources: Fundación Casitas de la Providencia, Medellín, 1964
Quality of information: Approximate

H	Health	Bus (solid line)
PO	Post Office	Rapid Transit
SS	Social Services	(broken line)

Pk	Parking	Ch	Church
P	Police	R	Recreation
F	Fire Department	L	Library
S	School	U	University

VILLA SOCORRO, Medellín View up hill taken from the winding road. Walls predominate, and little of the dwelling garden courts is seen. (1968)

Circulation: The central vehicular road is a bus route with a frequent service; access to all plots not facing the road is via walkways perpendicular to the slope.

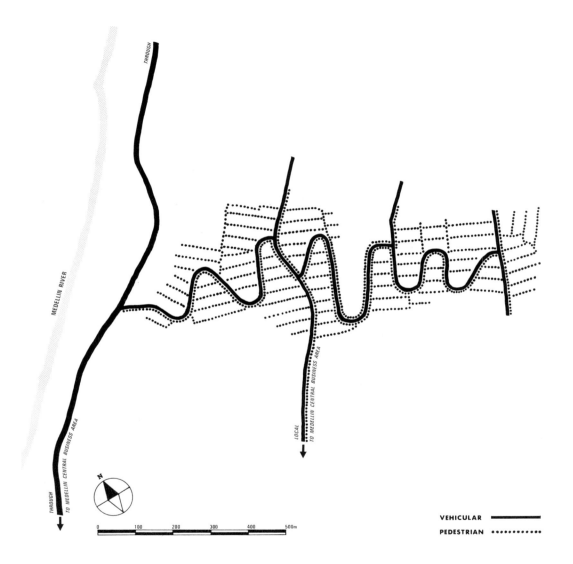

VILLA SOCORRO, Medellín
LOCALITY CIRCULATION PATTERN
Source: Estimate, Horacio Caminos, 1967
Quality of information: Accurate

VEHICULAR ━━━━
PEDESTRIAN •••••••••••

The chart illustrates the approximate availability of utilities and services at four levels: no provision at all, very limited or occasional, generally available but inadequate, and adequate or normal service.

Quality of information: Approximate

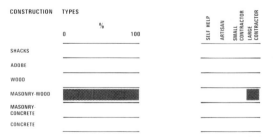

The main dwellings' construction types were grouped as follows: SHACK, ADOBE, WOOD, WOOD AND MASONRY, MASONRY AND CONCRETE, CONCRETE. The main characteristics of these types are described in the introduction.

The building industry was divided into the following groups: SELF-HELP, ARTISAN, SMALL CONTRACTOR, LARGE CONTRACTOR.

The chart shows (1) approximate percentage of each construction type within the total number of dwellings and (2) building group that generally produces each type.

Quality of information: Approximate

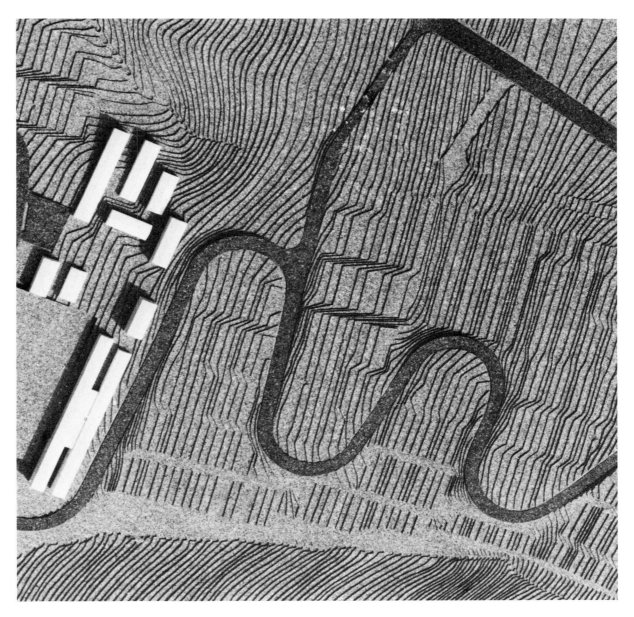

VILLA SOCORRO, Medellín
LOCALITY SEGMENT
400 m × 400 m; scale: 1:2500
Model of raw site showing topography, main circulation layout

Locality Segment: All plots and dwelling units are identical in area and type, but because the rectangular grid does not conform to the circulation system, there is a relatively high proportion of unused space that has no specific purpose.

LOCALITY SEGMENT

AREAS

PRIVATE OWNERSHIP	Hectares	Percentage
Dwelling Lots	3.81	36.71
Commercial	0.10	0.96
Industrial	—	—
PUBLIC OWNERSHIP		
Community Centers, Parks Playground, Schools	4.07	39.21
Streets—Parking	0.88	8.48
Pedestrian Walks	1.52	14.64
Total	10.38	100.00

DENSITIES	Number	Hectares	N/Ha
Lots	397	10.38	38.25
Dwelling Units	397	10.38	38.25
Families	397	10.38	38.25
People	2183	10.38	210.31
(5.5 People/Family)			

Quality of information: Approximate

VILLA SOCORRO, Medellín
LOCALITY SEGMENT PLAN
Sources: Fundación Casitas de la Providencia, Medellín, 1964
Quality of information: Accurate

SELECTED BLOCK

AREAS

PRIVATE OWNERSHIP		Hectares	Percentage
Dwelling Lots			
Commercial		0.68	48.57
Industrial			

PUBLIC OWNERSHIP			
Community Center, Parks		0.10	7.14
Playground, Schools			
Streets—Parking		0.30	21.43
Pedestrian Walks		0.32	22.86
	Total	1.40	100.00

DENSITIES	Number	Hectares	N/Ha
Lots	71	1.40	50.7
Dwelling Units	71	1.40	50.7
Families	71	1.40	50.7
People	390.5	1.40	278.9
(5.5 People/Family)			

CIRCULATION RATIO

$$\frac{\text{Circulation Length} = 525 \text{ m}}{\text{Area} \qquad = 1.40 \text{ Ha}} = 375 \text{ m/Ha}$$

Selected block is the area enclosed by the broken line on the Locality Segment plan.

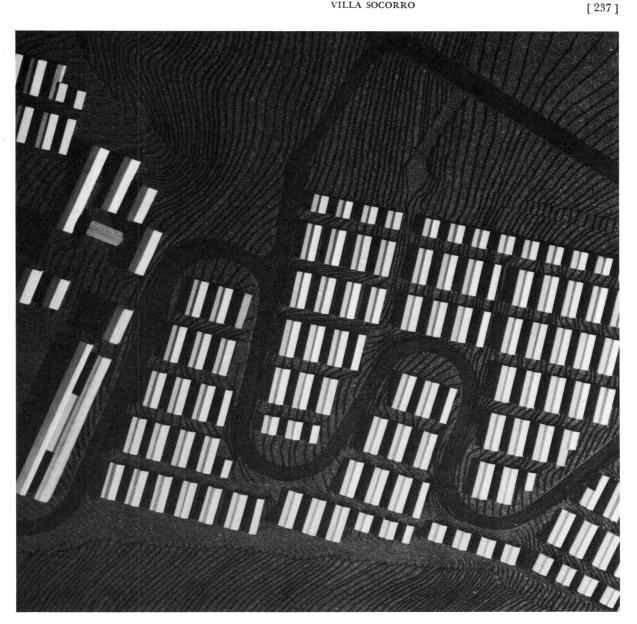

VILLA SOCORRO, Medellín
LOCALITY SEGMENT
400 m × 400 m; scale: 1:2500
Model of developed site showing existing buildings and streets

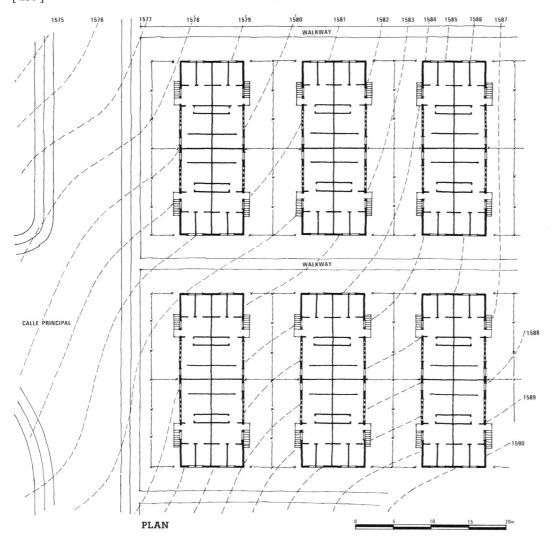

PLAN

0   5   10   15   20m

Dwelling Group: The standardized dwelling units and plots are arranged in blocks of four, sharing the back and (with the additional room) the side party walks and footings. On the site it is not immediately evident that the same unit is repeated throughout; this is because angles and levels of view are changing constantly, and also because many houses have been redecorated by the occupants.

VILLA SOCORRO, Medellín
DWELLING GROUP
Sources: Fundación Casitas de la Providencia, Medellín, 1964
Quality of information: Accurate

VILLA SOCORRO, Medellín Barbershop; dressmaker. Small corner shops are scattered along the winding road. (1968) (*opposite page, top left*)

Pedestrian street. A corner shop shows its walk-in window topped by a canopy to protect customers. (1968) (*opposite page, bottom left*)

A row of dwellings. Dwellings are grouped in blocks of four, to minimize walls. They are stepped to follow the contours. (1968) (*opposite page, top right*)

A pedestrian street and dwelling seen from the winding road. (1968) (*opposite page, bottom right*)

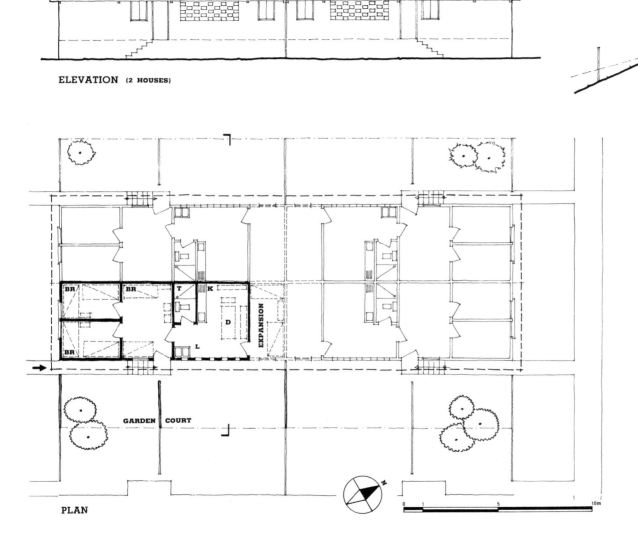

ELEVATION (2 HOUSES)

SECTION (2 HOUSES)

PLAN

DWELLING-UNIT AREAS

	m^2	%
Living (BR, DR, D, LR, K, C)	35.19	81.84
Service (T, L)	1.51	3.51
Circulation	—	—
Walls	6.30	14.65
Other	—	—
Total Unit Area:	43.00	100.00

Total Lot Area: $8.00 \times 12.00 = 96.00$ m², private use

LR	Living Room	**K**	Kitchen
DR	Dining Room	**L**	Laundry
D	Dining	**T**	Toilet—Bathroom
BR	Bedroom	**C**	Closet

VILLA SOCORRO, Medellín
TYPICAL DWELLING
Sources: Fundación Casitas de la Providencia, Medellín, 1964
Quality of information: Approximate

VILLA SOCORRO, Medellín View down hill shows roofs and the garden courts of the dwellings. Small openings in the roofs are for ventilation. (1968)

VILLA SOCORRO, Medellín

Dwelling

Design and development: Private foundation; instant development.

Year of construction: 1963.

Type of dwelling: Single-family semidetached house in a group of four.

Approximate number of people per unit: 6 people.

Approximate dwelling area per person: 7.16 sq. m.

Layout: Dwelling has single entrance; no corridors, rooms are used for circulation.

Facilities: Kitchen, dining area, and laundry in one room; toilet; garden of 45 sq. m; dwelling can be extended by the addition of one 8 sq. m bedroom.

Components: Windows are minimized; a perforated wall in the kitchen, instead of window, provides ventilation, security, and some light. In this case the perforated wall is protected from rain by the roof overhang.

Type of construction: Masonry bearing walls of a combination of bricks and ceramic hollow tiles, 10 × 20 × 40 centimeters; roof of corrugated asbestos cement sheets on wood beams.

For comparison see the following dwellings: El Agustino (Hill), which has a similar topography; El Gallo, which is the only other dwelling of the Latin American examples designed by "experts."